FUNCTIONAL FEMINISM

AN APOLITICAL GUIDE TO WOMEN'S EMPOWERMENT

DANA BROOKS

Published by Vervante, Inc.

Printed in the United States of America
Dana Brooks
Functional Feminism: An Apolitical Guide to Women's Empowerment
ISBN: 978-1-64775-274-3

Disclaimer

This book is written for women and girls and men who support their empowerment. It is sold with the understanding that the publisher and author are not engaged in rendering medical, legal, financial or other professional services. If professional services or expert assistance is required, the services of a specialist should be sought. The purpose of this book is to share the author's knowledge and experience in order to educate and inspire. The author and Vervante, Inc. shall have neither liability nor responsibility to any person or entity with respect to any loss or damage caused, or alleged to have been caused, directly or indirectly, by the information contained in this book.

Cover artwork courtesy of Robin Colucci.

Table of Contents

"Functional Feminism is a smart title for this frank and uncompromising—but never self-consciously PC—look at male-female relations. I'd hate to have to argue with Dana Brooks in a courtroom or social setting." ~ Bill Cotterell, Retired journalist, *Tallahassee Democrat*, UPI

"Dana's experiences with race early in life shaped her to focus on where we are alike as human beings with human needs. Learning of her upbringing and experiences explains to me why she is who she is, and why she has been so successful in her advocacy for fair and equal treatment of people." ~ Dianne Williams-Cox, Tallahassee City Commissioner

"The chapter for men really meant something to me. (Dana) saw me. That matters and if we are going to make progress and move forward as gender, and gender roles, become more fluid and more dynamic, we all need to see one another a lot better. Count me in as a functioning feminist!" ~ Len Northfield, Counsellor / Therapist at Zenbird Counselling Services

"Dana is a force to be reckoned with, a powerhouse of determination and passion, a warrior for women and children, and a voice for women who may know that they deserve it all, but may not know where to start." ~ Amy Kane, LMFT

For Whitney

May the world be easier, kinder, and fairer for you.

Acknowledgments

I've been pregnant twice in my life – once with my daughter, Whitney, and again with this damn book. I am so happy to finally be in the delivery room. But I didn't get here by myself. So, I appreciate your indulgence while I thank some people who probably never believed they'd be holding this book in their hands.

To my women law partners, Rose Kasweck, Kimmy Hogan, and Carrie Roane. Each of you informed this book in a meaningful way. I am in awe of you. I know what you have taken on professionally, despite your other obligations. The way you live your lives with such grace, dignity, and enthusiasm inspires me to be better. You are all so unique, so complex, and so damn smart. You are productive beyond measure, which motivates me to do more. I am thankful you chose to help others by joining our law firm and I am honored to call you my friends. Rose, I particularly thank you for letting me love you. You're my prickly pear.

To my heroes and sheroes, most of whom didn't realize I'd given them that job. I identified you. I watched you. I emulated you until I figured out who I was. Thank you for the guidance you never knew you gave me.

To Alana Weatherstone, Elizabeth Hughes, and all of the mentees I've served over the years. I've learned more from you than you ever learned from me. Thank you for reaching out. We all go through life trying to do the right thing and help as many people as we can, but it sure feels great when we see it come to fruition. Everything you do and everything you become makes me proud to be a small part of it. I am as excited as you are about your future. You two are like daughters to me and I cannot wait to sit in the background watching you take the stage.

To Robin Colucci, my book coach, and her editorial team, Otis Fuqua, Aubrey Polliard, and Dawn Mena. I thank you especially because I am one hard dog to keep under the porch. You have the patience of Job and the wisdom of the Magi. Thank you for pulling me out of the weeds, keeping me motivated, and helping me organize all this content in cogent order. Robin, you are much more of a friend than a coach, and I look forward to many years of seeing what you do and who you inspire! Otis, thank you for your insights on masculinity from your unique perspective. It always helps to hear from the people you are trying to address. Aubrey and Dawn, you kept me on track and your taste is flawless. Thank you for turning a dream into a reality.

To Maya Hoffman, a young woman whose name you'll want to know. Thank you for consulting with me and providing your perspective as a young woman. It's my hope that you'll have less complete and utter bullshit to deal with as you grow and become who you want to be in this big world. You have no limits.

To my husbands. What an unusual club you find yourselves in through no intentional effort. If after reading this you each feel you were truly special to me, that you were "the one," and that you were seen, heard, and deeply loved, my work here is done. Because at that time in my life, you were. I wish you happiness beyond any we experienced together. You deserve it.

To my parents. You had no idea what you were doing when I came into your lives and God knows it would have gone infinitely better had you been gifted with an easier child. I've probably learned the most from the two of you and though that wasn't easy for me, I thank you for it. It made me who I am, and I am pretty awesome.

To my dear sweet friends and COVID crew. I laugh now when I think of how many times I've told you I was "working on my book," yet no book materialized. Still, you never wavered in your support. You got me off the couch when I was at my lowest and reminded me just how great it feels to laugh again. I love you to the moon and back. Kristen Heyser, Caitlin Timineri, Bill Heyser, Gordy Cox, Ray Shashaty, Karen Thomas, Greg Tish.

To Layne Smith, a longtime friend and advisor. Thank you for "the talk" that very sad day in August 2018. It was the impetus for the new life I've created, and I owe you a debt of gratitude for your candor, time, and genuine concern. My love for you and your family runs deeper than you know. You've always been an example to me of "getting it right." Thank you for that.

To Jim Alves and Wade Nettles who came into my life at the same time and for the same reason – to get me mentally and physically well. You've become so much more to me than professional guides. My life has been deeply enriched by your presence in it and I thank you.

To Kelly Overstreet Johnson, who unwittingly motivated me to apply to law school. That one choice forever changed my life by granting me the autonomy, agency, and frankly, money, to live a life I never dreamed of. I only hope I can inspire as many women as you have to go for the brass ring, with the unyielding belief that they'll reach it.

To Amy Kane, Len Northfield, Bill Cotterell, Commissioner Dianne Williams-Cox, who took the time to read this manuscript, offer constructive feedback and simply encourage me in this journey. Thank you for the praise. It means everything to me.

To Kira Derryberry for indulging me and being THE BEST photographer in Tallahassee. I hope to be seen through your eyes.

To Jimmy Fasig. There are no words. From randomly texting me at 3:00 a.m. "We're going to be rich!" to actually making that happen. I always believed in you, though you often scared the shit out of me. But beyond the firm's success, beyond the thousands of people we've served, beyond the money, you showed me what it really means to be rich. To have just one person who has your back. To have just one person who gets you. To have just one person who loves you unconditionally, and in fact, despite all your warts and literal bruises. That, my friend, is a rich person. I am rich. Because of you.

Finally, to Whitney Claire, my sweetest potato. Being your mother is the only job that has ever mattered. It has my full attention, even and especially when you don't see it. Nothing matters more. But knowing when to protect you and when to watch you go your own way has been my greatest challenge. I can give you so more than my parents gave me and I struggle with what is healthy. We will figure this out together. You are the bright light that keeps me moving forward and my love for you is boundless. You make me so proud.

Foreword

When I began practicing law in the early 80s, the local bar association had hundreds of male members, but less than a dozen women lawyer members. Very few women came to meetings, so it was not unusual for there to be only a couple women lawyers in attendance. At the time, women were still struggling with what a female lawyer should look like. Is it acceptable to wear make-up and fashionable attire, or do you have to wear a navy-blue suit and try to look like the men? How do you respond when a male judge and bailiff have a discussion in front of you, debating whether or not you were the "cutest little lady lawyer they had ever seen?" Questions that, sadly, women lawyers must still contend with today, as Dana recounts in her book.

I remember making a presentation with another woman lawyer to female law students about dressing for success. The other woman lawyer spoke first. Her advice: no make-up, nail polish, or jewelry, and do not draw attention to your appearance.

Well, I went next and what did I look like that day? A blue silk dress, pearls, make-up, and nail polish, of course. I was all about being myself and not trying to fit in with what a stereotypical male lawyer looked like.

Meeting Dana at a Tallahassee Bar meeting in the 90s, not hiding her femininity, but embracing it, I knew I'd met someone who understood the challenge and responsibility of being a woman in what many believe (then and now) is a male-dominated field. I soon learned we had a lot in common. We both grew up in the south, and were well schooled in "being southern" and what that entailed, especially for women. Did you cross the line in how "opinionated" or "demanding" you were? Where did that fine line lie?

We both had to find our way, managing the responsibilities of motherhood in tandem with our career ambitions. When I decided to run for president of The Florida Bar, I was a married mother of 2-and-a-half-year-old twins. People thought I was crazy, but I had a plan.

When Dana began her second career as a lawyer, she had a young daughter, and her then husband was against her going to law school. People thought she was crazy too, but Dana also had a plan.

In our careers, Dana and I have supported each other and other women as much as we can. We've both had male mentors, and while we wouldn't trade them for the world, the opportunity to be mentored by (or to give mentorship as) a woman is critical. A female mentor can offer a woman a unique perspective, support and encouragement. Women are different, and their challenges are different.

From the outside, it seems only natural that Dana has achieved such heights. She relishes in her role as the beautiful blonde on local billboards and a TV talk show, the up-and-coming female trial lawyer. She is comfortable in her skin: her height, her long blonde hair, her feminine attire. But hard work and determination were behind her seemingly effortless rise to success. In *Functional Feminism*, Dana shares some of what she has learned on her journey to becoming the financially secure and successful lawyer you see today. In reading Dana's book, I felt much of the same angst she describes so directly.

Successful women aren't born successful. They achieve success through hard work and there are many disappointments along the way. Life isn't fair. It isn't easy. So if you aren't successful upon your first effort, keep trying. If you want it badly enough, it is worth the effort. As Dana points out, real success comes from freedom. Monetary success often allows freedom of choice, but having the ability to make those choices is what it is all about. Dana offers many lessons to help you achieve this success. Perhaps my favorite is Dana's plea not to disparage other women. It is OK to have different points of view. Stand up for yourself and each other. Don't bully. Don't be afraid to fail–put yourself out there. To lend my voice to Dana's already growing call: ladies–be there for each other! We can do this!

~ Kelly Overstreet Johnson is a practicing lawyer and mediator in Tallahassee, Florida. She is a past president of The Florida Bar (the third largest bar in the country). In addition to numerous bar activities during her almost 40 year career, she treasures her involvement and leadership in the Tallahassee Women Lawyers (president – 1984) and as the first woman president of the Tallahassee Bar Association (1989-90). Kelly is married to a lawyer (now happily retired), and the mother of twin college-age daughters.

Introduction

Feminism is an uncomfortable word. People cringe when they hear it. Over the years, it's come to be associated with unattractive, strident, intransigent women. Even women who promote feminist causes, veritable paragons of female empowerment, sometimes bristle at the word. "Oh, I'm not a *feminist*. I'm all for women's rights and equality, but please, do not call me a feminist."

I don't mean to minimize the great feminist advances of recent years. Women are reporting sexual misconduct more than ever, and at last, men are starting to believe us. Women are rising into more and more c-suites, public offices, and decision-making roles. Women are empowering ourselves to make our own choices and set our own standards for the lives we want to lead. If you took a poll, most of the country would express strong support for gender equality and a willingness to work and sacrifice towards it. Yet for so many, feminism still carries a negative connotation.

Throughout my life, it has been a struggle to be a feminist. When I was a girl, adults discouraged me from talking about the Equal Rights Amendment (ERA) and exploring feminist ideas, likely for fear I'd never get a man to marry me. As a named partner and owner of a law firm in a male-dominated field, competitors and supporters alike have told me to downplay those feminist ideals, focus more on law, and worry less about protecting and promoting women and girls. They feared it was too divisive and would hurt my business. So, for me, being a feminist is hard work. The stigma the label carries has only made it harder.

I understand some fears surrounding the word "feminist." It doesn't have the best track record. When I grew up, in the second wave of feminism, the word represented a far greater departure from the norm than it does today. In the 1970s and '80s, being a feminist meant facing extreme pushback from your peers, with society labeling you as a bra-burning, hairy arm-pitted man-hater. It often meant relocating to a new city or neighborhood to be around like-minded folks. You couldn't expect to be a feminist and remain in polite society.

As such, the second wave of feminism left many behind. If taking up the cause was so radical it entailed becoming subject to even more prejudice and discrimination, where did this leave women of color, queer and trans women, and women with disabilities? If being a feminist meant being a socialist radical, what room was there for women with conservative values? Where was the feminism for women who embraced a traditional gender role? For women who wanted to make a home for their husband and raise their children? Feminism has excluded many in the past, and we still have the scars to prove it.

The word "feminist" itself also poses hindrances. Femininity is built right into it. A lot of people don't identify with femininity, or don't want to call attention to it in themselves. It's a gendered word, in a world where gender as a concept is on the decline. Worse, society punishes femininity through a mountain of social constructs, rooted in male insecurity.

In short, the word "feminist" has fallen short of its lofty ideals. Not every feminist can afford to be a martyr, and not every feminist fits the crunchy-granola stereotype. Not every feminist is feminine, and not every feminist is female. In this book, I use feminine modifiers to include people assigned that gender at birth and those who identify as female, but feminism can be embraced by everyone, regardless of gender identity. And that's not only okay, it's necessary. Feminism can only exist if there's a place for everyone in it. And I mean *everyone*.

Changing our culture and policies to honor femininity and be fairer to women demands we come together. This is not to equate unity with uniformity, as we mustn't forget the specific challenges that come with each of our identities, but we cannot allow a patriarchal society to use those differences to divide us. At this point in history, the time has come for a sea change. Let's look for global commonalities as we work together to surmount common enemies. There is a place for everyone in this wave of feminism.

It is my hope that by adding "functional" to idea of feminism, we can remove some of the cultural venom feminism has accrued, open the movement to all (I see you feminist-curious folks out there), and emphasize what's most important in feminism and in life: getting shit done. Consider this book the case for modern feminism – functional feminism, if you will. I hope to enlist your help in promoting and defending it.

This book is also a celebration of womanhood. Being a woman is a beautiful thing, but there are those who still think otherwise, almost like it's an affliction. They believe that women didn't win the birth lotto; it sucks to be us. All over the world, women are complacent, accepting second-class citizenship, blind or inured to their mistreatment. In the simplest of terms, *fuck that*. It is high time we all take a step back, look at ourselves, at the women in our lives, and celebrate. Women are awesome!

At its core, feminism is about *choice*. You can be a feminist and still hold a traditional role in a nuclear family. You can do whatever you want. That's the entire point of *functional* feminism. It's not about burning bras or rejecting marriage and children in favor of education and career. It's about having the full freedom and autonomy to make informed decisions about how you want to live your life. It's about honoring and empowering yourself to choose what works for you, and extending that same kindness to everyone else. There is no one way to be a good feminist; there is only your way. I hope this book will help you find it, or at the very least, make it so you don't recoil every time you hear the word. Rather, I hope it becomes an idea you can embrace with pride. I believe everyone should be a feminist!

The following chapters encompass the lessons I've learned on my journey of self-actualization and professional success. Read them in whatever order you prefer. If you're a man, I recommend starting with chapter seven, so you begin with an understanding of how you fit into the preceding chapters. Please note, in describing gender dynamics, I use the words "women" and "men" for rhetorical ease and readability, not to reinforce the gender binary, or to exclude nonbinary people from the conversation. When writing about marriage and romantic relationships, I describe a monogamous, heterosexual relationship, simply because that is my orientation. This is not to ignore other relationship types, but to write with authenticity from my own experience, without interpolating my experience onto others. Finally, there are eight strategically placed fucks in this book. Well, nine, if you count this one. Be forewarned.

I hope you enjoy it.

CHAPTER 1

Use Everything You've Got

I n 2019, I spoke on work-life balance at a marketing and management conference for attorneys. I presented on the featured "Women's Day" of the conference, and had to (got to?) follow Gloria Allred, renowned women's rights lawyer. I actually got to ride down in the elevator with her (#FangirlMoment) and she was remarkably congenial.

At the conference, Ms. Allred explained her motivations for going to law school and spending a lifetime fighting for women. She spoke about being raped at gunpoint. It was in Acapulco, Mexico, in the mid-1960s, when abortion was illegal. She'd already had a child, was divorced, and in college. She chose to terminate the pregnancy. This led to her having a back-alley abortion in a bathtub from an unlicensed provider. She started hemorrhaging and developed a fever that soared to 106 degrees Fahrenheit. She went to the hospital, where other women were experiencing similar post-abortion complications. For days, she was seriously ill. She almost died. Once she was out of the woods and it looked like she would pull through, she told us, one judgmental nurse said to her, "This should teach you a lesson."

Ironically, the man who strong-arm raped Ms. Allred that summer had been a local physician. She said she never reported the rape because people told her due to his stature in the community, nothing would come of it. I can't imagine the number of women that man brutalized over the years without experiencing any consequences.

Meeting Gloria Allred and hearing her speak was a bucket list item for me for a few reasons. First, she's brave as fuck. I cannot fathom what she's endured. She is one tough broad. Second, like me, men have brutalized her, yet she refuses to cower and identify as a victim. She found a way to outmatch their physical strength by using her knowledge of the law and made a name for herself as a preeminent women's rights attorney, pushing past her circumstances and surpassing even her loftiest goals. Third, she has dedicated her life to fighting for victimized women. It's not just her job; it's her mission. Ms. Allred inspired me to think long and hard about my mission, and if I was doing everything I could to advance it.

Into the Fray: Refocusing My Practice on Helping Victimized Women

Like Gloria Allred, I too had a life-changing event that motivated me to focus my practice on protecting women—the 2018 Kavanaugh hearings.

At the time, I was speaking all over the country on female empowerment, work-life balance, and marketing and branding for women. Meanwhile, in my personal law practice, I was suing doctors and hospitals for negligence. Being a medical malpractice attorney was intellectually stimulating, but I never felt good about suing a doctor because they'd had a bad day. The doctors took it way too personally, and it wasn't gratifying, suing people who are trying to do so much good in the world. Then the Kavanaugh hearings happened, and making sure my work addresses the challenges women face felt more important than ever.

Watching the Kavanaugh hearings on television gave me a newfound appreciation for the toll litigation takes on all involved parties, and I decided it was time to refocus. From then on, I determined I would only do work that protected women and girls, and only go after the people who really had it coming–the predators. It didn't take long before I realized this shift would make me a very busy lawyer.

I'm passionate about protecting women, in part because I've experienced sexual assault. More than once. I've endured strong-arm stranger rape, and boys and men who just would not accept "no" who harassed me until they overpowered me, or I just got tired and gave in. I'm not ashamed of this, but I don't lead with it, either. I don't want that to be my story or what people first think of when they hear my name.

I have no burning desire to seek out and punish these men. I hope they've changed and matured, and I hope that when they look back on their behavior, they're ashamed of it. But let one of those bastards get nominated to the highest court in the land, where he will be one of the nine people in this country with the power to decide what I, my daughter, and other women can do with our own bodies, and I will *ruin* him.

Why Women Don't Report: The Deck is Stacked Against Us

Coverage of the Brett Kavanaugh Supreme Court confirmation hearings revealed one fact we all knew, but never wanted to admit: just about every woman out there has a #MeToo story. I knew it long before it became the most talked about matter of 2018. I've been a woman on this planet for over five decades–it's impossible *not* to know. Every human being paying attention knows this shit happens, and with far more frequency than we hear about. For that reason, I find the knee-jerk reaction to reports of past predatory behavior—"Why is she just now reporting it?"—a boldfaced attempt to make an excuse to cover up a crime.

I'd think the reasons women don't report would be obvious, but let's break it down.

First, being a victim of sexual misconduct is a fact of life for women. Every one of us has had at least one experience where we just choked it down and never said or did anything about it. If we reported every sexually-charged nickname, every gross come-on, every taunt, every unwanted touch (which is actually a "battery" under the law), every "advancement opportunity" offered that was conditioned upon our doing something uncomfortable and irrelevant to the position, we'd have little time to do much else.

Then there is the second layer of the burden—our society disbelieves victims of sexual assault, and women in general, by design. If women did report every actionable offense, we would come across as the oversensitive, shrill, hysterical females society makes us out to be. It's the ultimate irony—because this behavior is so pervasive, if we reported every instance of it, we would water down its effects. If everyone has experienced something, it can't really be that bad, right? This leads those in power to spin women's reports of sexual misconduct as further proof of our second-class citizenry, saying we can't even "take a compliment" or hang out with men without "ruining all the fun."

When women think about reporting bad behavior, we see the prospect of further victimization. Who needs that? No, women want to put that experience behind them and move on. After something life-threatening like rape, or a fight for their professional lives where the stakes are enormous, women are thankful just to have survived. Revenge and retribution don't even enter the equation.

Women are conditioned to blame ourselves. We receive messages our whole lives reminding us we are not as important, not as smart, and not as competent, so when something bad happens to us, it must be our fault. Instead of thinking about how an asshole should pay for his bad behavior, a woman ruminates over whether she did something to mislead the letch, or if she should have worn a different outfit, or not gone to that party. Why would any woman think she can withstand the judgment of others when she's already struggling with her own self-doubt, and blaming herself for her own victimization?

Third, regardless of when she reports it, the general expectation is that no one will believe one woman's outcry. Not without clear video proof. Even with DNA evidence, the conversation shifts to consent; and some still believe consent is mere acquiescence after a period of protest or on a victim's realization of the power imbalance between herself and the predator.

Worse, few will believe several women telling the same story about the same man if that man is not a total bottom feeder. Even then, he needs to have past accusations of a similar nature, lest people accuse women of mistaking his identity or conspiring against the poor fella'. When there are multiple accusations against one man, instead of thinking he must be a malicious actor, our conditioning leads us to be suspicious of the women accusers. We look for themes and commonalities among them. Are they old, fat, or ugly? Are they just miserable hags who couldn't get laid or find a husband? Are they just trash, anyway? Or maybe they're just crazy, hysterical females. Whatever it is, women accusers never receive a beneficial default judgment, yet people will contort themselves to defend even the most indefensible behavior in a man they don't even know.

If the accused "has a family," or "a reputation to worry about," or is "an influential person in the community," the burden of proof on women is even greater. An army of women can tell the same story, and instead of believing them, people will lump them together into a category of money-hungry, fame-seeking opportunists. Instead of thinking, "How awful that these women have suffered and this predator has gotten away with it for so long," society's first impulse is to wonder how much money the "victims" are suing for, or how much of an advance they've gotten on their book deals. It's maddening, which is why so many women continue to suck it up as an unfortunate but unavoidable part of being female.

Law enforcement officers have told me—a known feminist trial lawyer—that unless it's a stranger committing a strong-arm rape, they don't consider sexual assault a "real crime." Literally. Instead of empowering victims to seek justice, they try their best to persuade them not to bring charges. They scare victims with the parade of nightmares that are sure to result from reporting the abuse—damage to her reputation, online harassment, having to drop out of school or relocate, lack of career options, etc.

To cops who think like that, it's impossible for a man to rape his wife or girlfriend. To them, there is no such thing as date rape. That's just a bad night, and the remedy is to not go out with that guy again, or maybe not "let yourself" be alone with guys you don't know well, or maybe dress a little more conservatively, or maybe don't get "sloppy drunk," even if the drink you had happened to contain Rohypnol. Not once do we hear, "You can never be drunk enough for it to be okay for someone to rape you," or "There's no way to dress that makes it okay for a man to take what he wants from you without your full consent." That attitude from law enforcement reinforces a woman's self-doubt, reminding her it's either no big deal or her fault entirely.

Finally, before we judge women for "not reporting sooner," let's examine exactly what possible benefit a woman might get for doing so. What do we get for reporting sexual misconduct?

We see the negatives—stigma, self-doubt, accusations of having "asked for it," "let it happen to you," or of "ruining a good man's life." Are there any positives? What about those big lawsuit settlements and book deals? What about the satisfaction of seeing these predators arrested, tried, and jailed for their crimes? Surely that makes it all worthwhile.

Well, not if you are a rational thinker. A rational thinker knows victims have no control over whether law enforcement will arrest someone for sexual assault or if the state attorneys will prosecute those cases. Even when there is an arrest, prosecution, and conviction, the sanctions range from a slap on the wrist to hard time. None of that puts the victim in the position she was in prior to the assault. At most, it punishes the predator, and in theory, keeps him from victimizing others, for a while. For women who choose not to report, the thought of allowing a monster to continue hurting women is yet another burden they have to bear.

There must be a monetary payoff in suing for sexual assault, then. Wrong again. Most bad guys don't have big insurance policies to cover their deliberate criminal acts, nor are they sitting on piles of collectible cash or assets. There are the Bill Cosbys and Harvey Weinsteins of the world, with more than enough money to compensate the victims of their crimes, but they are exceptions to the rule. Most insurance only covers negligent or careless behavior, not intentional acts or crimes, and many specifically exclude sexual misconduct. A woman almost never collects a settlement straight from the bad guy. Usually, she has to collect from someone with vicarious responsibility for the wrongdoer, like their employer or a property owner.

Harassment often occurs in work settings, where employment contracts and arbitration agreements favor the more powerful parties, the predator and his employer, while limiting the rights of the injured party and her ability to collect damages. Even if the injured party is free to sue, civil lawsuits can only compensate women for what they've already lost, not the far-reaching consequences this career interruption may have on her overall earnings and upward mobility.

Assuming a woman musters the fortitude to bring a civil lawsuit to court, how would she quantify the effect of sexual assault on her life? If her employer fired her or she had to leave her job, chances are she's gone out and found another one, because she's a woman, and she and her kids, if she has them, need to eat. Getting a new job hurts her claim for damages, because she's already begun to mitigate them.

7

Getting another job does not make a woman whole, though. Most women make lateral transfers or take demotions to get out of bad work environments. In doing so, a woman loses all of her institutional knowledge, as it's nontransferable to her new employment environment. She'll have to start all over again learning the culture, building alliances, and finding the ins for promotion and advancement. Had she remained in her position and continued on course, she'd be much farther along with regard to both financial and promotional opportunities. It's a hidden cost with almost incalculable damage. This results in women almost never receiving compensation for the long-term negative effects of having to flee an environment of harassment and abuse through a lateral transfer or demotion. Again, women are expected to suck it up as part of life for a second-class citizen.

Many women claim past employers or coworkers have "blackballed" them for reporting sexual harassment. They say their name has become toxic to prospective employers, and that they've lost good jobs they were well-qualified for because someone they used to work with bad-mouthed them for speaking up. While sexual harassment happens often, it is almost impossible for a woman to prove unless she has witnesses willing to testify they would have hired or given her a lucrative deal, had someone not blackballed her for reporting sexual assault. No one's going to admit doing that, as it puts them in the same bad light as the original predator.

But let's get back to the numbers. Say a woman misses a year of work where she would have earned $100,000. If she receives that amount in a settlement, she first has to pay her attorneys' fees, in most cases one-third of the settlement. If the case is litigated, 40 percent of the settlement goes to her attorneys. Even the biggest-hearted attorneys don't work for free. Next, she pays the expenses of the litigation, such as filing fees, deposition transcripts, and travel. Since at least part of her compensation is for lost wages, she will owe income tax on that amount of the settlement. After all those deductions, she likely receives about 35 to 40 percent of her actual lost wages. Worse yet, to get any compensation at all, she has to sign a confidentiality agreement containing strong financial sanctions should she divulge the terms of the settlement to anyone for any reason without a court order.

In the end, after experiencing a predator's victimization, standing up for herself, and bringing a lawsuit to hold the wrongdoer accountable, she ends up with a fraction of what the harassment cost her, and she can't even tell anyone about the mistreatment. Not such a sexy deal, is it? And that's not to mention enduring a complete character assassination for the two or three years it takes to get a case to the point where it's ripe for settlement.

Long before settlement, the defense attorney of the accused will have spoken with every person who has something bad to say about the plaintiff. They'll have combed through her social media posts for anything at all controversial or unflattering. They'll have contacted every co-worker, friend and former lover she's ever had a spat with. The defense will have taken that negative evidence and blown it up so big it's visible from space, and trotted it into the courtroom to convince the arbitrator, judge, or jury, that this woman is not a credible plaintiff/victim/human being. In fact, they'll argue, this is all *her* fault. *She* is the one who victimized this fine, upstanding defendant, and it is *she* who the court should hold to account for the damage she's done. What this man and his family have endured is outrageous and we cannot allow women like her to use the judicial system to terrorize men who own businesses, create jobs, and have families to support.

That's right! These people typically countersue for slander, libel, intentional interference in business relationships, and anything else they think of to control the narrative, assume the victim stance, and demonize the plaintiff. So, while the victim is fighting to prosecute her claim, she'll also have to defend herself in a fictionalized counter lawsuit.

And that's only the liability aspect of the case. If the prosecution manages to establish the sexual harassment defendant is guilty of wrongful behavior, the victim must then establish the harm she's suffered. It's easy to demonstrate the value of lost income and benefits, but what about the mental pain, suffering, and loss of enjoyment of life resulting from sexual assault or harassment?

At this point, the defendant's attorneys will again come sniffing into the woman's life. They will use every questionable decision she's ever made, every one-night stand she's had, and every painful moment she's endured in her life, to show given her tortured past, this little harassment thing can't be what's really ruining her life. As cynical as people are, they tend to believe that narrative.

It ought to be clear to you by now, there's no million-dollar pain and suffering component to these cases, either. Juries tend to undervalue the victim's pain and suffering, if they value it at all. They'll justify it by saying, "This isn't the worst thing that ever happened to you, look at x, y, and z from your past." Or, "This happens to other women, too. How bad can it be?" Or the old, "Sister, life ain't fair. We all got problems and nobody's giving us any money for them."

By the end of litigation, the victim will have endured the most grueling, invasive questioning imaginable, under oath, sometimes for days. Her friends and family will be split on whether to support her or encourage her to walk away. Along the way, she will question many times whether she made the right decision and if it was all worth it. More likely than not, she will leave the entire process with a bad taste in her mouth, feeling even more cynical about the world than she did when she started.

Standing up for yourself in a legal environment can be so demoralizing, it's no wonder so few women put themselves through it, even when it could benefit other women. Often, it's simply too much for one already victimized woman to take on. God knows if a victim looks for support, she won't find many women who have successfully sued for sexual harassment, achieved a great victory, and moved on to live their best lives.

You might be thinking the good news is that at least when the accused is an "important person," all those podcasts, TV show interviews, and book deals make the entire ordeal all worthwhile. No. That's actually not true, either. While they may make a victim famous for a moment, they also bring them a lot of backlash. Relentless online and in-person harassment, threats to their families and their lives, having to relocate and go into hiding, having to hire security—it's nowhere near as glamorous as it sounds. Anybody want to trade places with Anita Hill? Monica Lewinsky? Dr. Christine Blasey-Ford? Didn't think so.

When victims report sexual misconduct, they face a minefield of challenges, both in and out of court. It's hell, and no woman puts herself and her family through that to get famous, rich, or become an author. She's doing it out of principle, for other women, and at great personal cost. The very minimum we should do is believe her.

Weapons in the Fight: Women's Unique Advantages

It's not all bad news, though. Because some brave women have walked this path before us, we can see a way through the forest now. The last message I want women reading this book to receive is that we're doomed to continue experiencing mistreatment with little hope for change, so suck it up and do nothing. That's simply not true.

While the brave women coming forward have made it just a little easier for the rest of us, we all possess unique skills and talents we can use in this fight. By embracing and optimizing these skills, we can help build a world where women receive better treatment in the workplace, society, and interpersonal relationships, to the benefit of women today and the girls and future generations of women to come.

It starts with walking into your power. Embracing everything you have right now and optimizing it for maximum performance. Use what you've got.

There is a lot of power and benefit to being a woman, but you've got to recognize, harness, and weaponize it. That begins with how you see yourself. It next develops into your brand, which is how the world sees you. Learn to be in control of your brand. If you don't know how to do that, look up and find leaders and mentors to guide you.

If you've never seen Gloria Allred in person, watch the Netflix documentary on her, *Seeing Allred*. Once you do, you'll see just how much force she packs into her small body. Standing next to her for photographs, I was about six foot one in my heels; we looked like we were two different species. Yet I didn't dwarf her. She owned all of her space. And it was all by design.

Ms. Allred is 78 years old and stands five foot two inches tall. And I do mean *tall*. She's known for wearing her signature red pantsuit, black blouse, and statement necklace. I've seen this suit up close. I don't know fashion well enough to postulate about the designer, but I do know fine clothing. The fabric caught the light without being shiny, and was heavy enough to lay flat but not so heavy it highlighted the bumpy areas. The suit pants were well-fitting and accentuated her curvy hips without clinging to them. The pants tapered at the knee, then flared a bit before falling approximately two millimeters from the floor, making Ms. Allred look as tall as possible without dragging on the floor. She no doubt wore the same shoes every time she wore that suit. The suit jacket, while a perfect fit for her tiny frame, had strong shoulders and a wide lapel, creating a much larger presence than the short, Chanel-type jackets many petites favor, hoping to emulate 1960s Jacqueline Kennedy grace. Clearly Ms. Allred wasn't trying to look ladylike or dainty. She was there to sit at the table, not set it.

Before she took the stage, big booming speakers played her upbeat intro music, leading into a ten-minute video overview

of her outstanding career achievements. It featured press conferences, interviews, and parts of *Seeing Allred*. The video ended
with a recap of her current efforts to seek justice for women
victimized by Bill Cosby, Harvey Weinstein, Donald Trump
and other famous, powerful, seemingly untouchable men. With
the music pumping, Ms. Allred ascended the stage and stood at
the podium to a roaring ovation. I had chills.

Imagine what the reaction would have been had she shown
up five foot two, age 78, in a floral print dress with a flared skirt,
flats, no make-up, and grown-out grey roots, with no music
build-up or video montage? How would the audience have
received her if she looked at her feet as she walked across the
stage, read from prepared notes, and never made eye contact
with the audience? No one would have listened to her. I know
it's not fair, but how we present ourselves matters. The good
news is how we go about it is 100 percent within our control.

I first learned this lesson in my third year of law school in a
class on trial strategy. It wasn't a course about substantive law,
it was about the 'psychology of trial practice,' which is code for
how to manipulate juries into doing what you want them to
do. Those were my favorite classes because they weren't taught
by academics far removed from the real practice of law, but by
real, practicing attorneys who were in the arena every day. Their
feedback I was interested in receiving.

At about six foot eight, our towering professor had attended
an Ivy League college on a basketball scholarship. He was
younger than the average law professor, and had a babyface.
Just like the five foot two woman who doesn't make eye contact
and wears a floral print dress and flats, his youthful face could
have been an impediment to gaining the respect he needed in
the courtroom.

This meant he had to use what he did have to offset what
he didn't. He talked about how he used his height to gain an
advantage. The class agreed, it was obvious he would tower over
everyone in just about any situation. But what about the rest
of us? What about those of us who aren't physical giants? Or

what about us women, who usually can't match a man's height and don't have his deep, commanding voice? He explained that every one of us has something unique that gives us an advantage we're just not optimizing it. He demonstrated this with a few classmates, starting with me.

I attended law school later in life, and was fifteen years older than my average classmate. Instead of seeming like the out-of-touch, old chick on campus, he noted that I came off as "sort of aloof."

My classmates agreed.

My "aloof" behavior, which was nothing more than a time-deprived, frazzled woman in her late 30s running a house, working, and raising three girls, came off as a put-together woman with extreme confidence. He pointed out what an immediate advantage my age and perceived confidence would afford me once I started practicing. No one would assume I was a new lawyer just by looking at me. That had never occurred to me. I was fighting imposter syndrome each day. My strategy was pure survival. I'd never thought to see myself as others did and amplify all that was good about it.

Next, he wanted to talk about my physicality. He pointed out that I, too, am above-average height. In heels (my native dress), I stand at about six feet tall. The average American male is five foot nine inches. He noted that my long blonde hair, while eye-catching, could be distracting or powerful, depending on how I used it.

Finally, he pointed out that being a woman afforded me wardrobe choices men do not have. Color, style, height–women have infinitely more options in dress than men. Instead of impersonating men in navy blue power suits with white blouses and understated pumps, our professor suggested we be our true selves while using our unique features to even the playing field. He encouraged us to consider our physicality in trying cases, along with our knowledge of the law and prowess with legal argument. He told us not to leave anything on the table. Use everything we've got.

Although this concept is universal, women are less likely to take risks to make up for their perceived deficits. Men enjoy much of their confidence because of how well life tends to go for them compared to women, which society reinforces every day in the amount of deference men receive simply because of their gender. Men are more likely to risk looking stupid or appearing silly to achieve a gain. Images of cowboys and industry tycoons all glorify men who take risks, making it much more comfortable for them. It's part of "being a man." And with more risk comes more reward. We women have to train ourselves to become comfortable taking risks, and that starts with our outward appearance—the face we show the world.

Once I started practicing law, I began to look at makeup, hair, and wardrobe as extra arrows in my quiver that my male competitors either didn't have or couldn't use as effectively. I've used it to develop a winning strategy which has served me well in my personal and professional life. Men can choose monotone power colors and tailor their clothes for maximum height and svelte-ness, but it's uncommon. Typically, they're not big on shopping or fashion trends, so they buy several suits at a time and wear those until they outgrow them or they wear them out. As long as a man feels it looked good when they bought it, they assume that it's true every time they wear it, regardless of the audience. Women tend to be agile. Men, not so much. Women know better. We know to always dress for our audience.

When my expert witness testifies on the stand, I wear a flesh-toned suit with flesh-colored pumps and demure jewelry. I pull my hair back and stay behind the podium. My intent is to become invisible. I want all eyes on my expert.

But when I cross-examine the expert witness for the opposition, I wear a red skirt suit, heels, and a statement necklace. I wear my hair big and down and put on full make-up. I want all eyes on me. If I am taller than the opposing expert (which I almost always am), I make a point to call him off the stand (it's almost always a man), and make him draw things and do live calculations for me in front of the jury, all while I tower over him and point out his errors. Eventually, the impression left with the jury is that I'm the one they need to listen to.

I use the courtroom as an example because it's easy to understand. Women have more power to harness than they realize. It can be through something as simple as commanding attention with how we dress, or something as nuanced as where to sit at a conference table for maximum effect. It's less about how you harness the power, than understanding how much of it is available to you. It's about seeing yourself as undefined and unlimited. It's about opening your mind to see yourself differently, which will necessarily result in others seeing and treating you differently.

One of the things I'm most proud of in my professional life is that in our firm, 57 percent of our partners are women and 75 percent of our shareholders are women. That's unheard of among private personal injury law firms our size. Each of my three female law partners and I have our own unique style and way of functioning in the male-dominated world in which we practice.

Sex Appeal vs. Sex

Women shouldn't leverage everything of value. We all know women who use their sexuality to try to leapfrog. Although your physical presence is powerful, being in control of it is different from using it in the wrong way—like sleeping your way to the top, or having affairs to get ahead. We're better than that. The modern woman loves and respects herself more than that, and she knows how short-sighted it is to leverage her sexuality.

It's short-sighted because it's trading on the least sustainable asset a woman has, while putting herself in a rotation to compete with younger and younger women. She sets a time-clock for herself, and that time always comes sooner than we think. Women who leverage their sexual assets to get ahead need to recognize that's not independence.

There is immense power in how we project ourselves. It becomes what others accept as our truth. One of my female law partners, Carrie Roane, is known for her sense of style. She follows current trends and enjoys couture. Everything she wears looks like it was made specifically to accentuate her physical features. She's always played sports and has a trim, athletic build. She has long, dark, beautiful hair and wouldn't consider cutting it to "look more professional," or because she's in her 40s now. It's her signature feature, and she owns it. She wears form-fitting clothes and spiky, edgy heels, even though she's five foot nine. She will wear leather to work as easily as she'll wear a floor length, red chiffon maxi skirt.

We first met because we used to litigate against each other. Although she was always pitted against me, I liked her. I loved her sense of style. I loved her confidence. At the time, she worked in a conservative Southern-style law firm, and I cannot imagine what they thought of her wardrobe choices. The fact that she didn't seem to care impressed the hell out of me. I knew she was a great lawyer, but I admired her as a woman role model as well.

The minute we convinced her to switch from defense to prosecution where she could do much more to help deserving people, I was thrilled. I knew our clients would feel empowered having such a female powerhouse representing them. She embraces her femininity but she doesn't downplay the aggressive, competitive nature of her personality, either.

But this wasn't always true for her. She confided to me that sometimes she still feels like the awkward teenager who got teased in high school for being flat-chested. She recalls wearing Catholic school uniforms as a child, and how stifling it felt to be unable to express her individuality through her own clothing choices. The ability to choose what she wears, from a wide array of choices, is powerful, and she knew that even as a child.

Yet nothing about her appearance or behavior suggests she's trying to leverage her gifts for improper gain. She doesn't sleep with people or suggest that's even possible in professional settings. She dresses for herself, not for what others think of her. She is who she is, and she wears it with pride. Even as an outlier in a room full of average-looking people, she doesn't apologize or cower to fit in. To do so, she is aware, would suggest there is something wrong with her. For her, fashion represents empowerment and the freedom to express herself. And she has mastered it. No one who meets her or observes her killer performances for her clients would ever suspect she'd had a moment of uncertainty about herself in her life.

Like Dorothy in Kansas, almost everything we need to succeed in life is already within our possession, we just haven't realized it yet. This is the concept people often describe as "occupying one's space." I hear this from women a lot right now. I hear words like, "I want to be seen. I want to be heard. I matter."

My immediate response is, "Well, of course you do! What on Earth ever made you think you didn't?!" Then I remember, "what on Earth" is their entire experience here. Every message they've heard since they were little girls has told them that they are here to play a supporting role, never the star.

Women have more power than we realize. Our only true limitations are the ones we place on ourselves, through negative self-talk, bowing to external influences, and holding on to faulty beliefs. Once I embraced all the things that are unique about myself and started treating them like the advantages they are, instead of fretting over how it made me "different" or "difficult," I began to occupy my space. I didn't start out that way, though.

I grew up with a single mother who worked full-time. I had next to no supervision as a young teen. My role models came from television, movies, and books, where again, most women were in a support position–someone's wife, mother, or employee. I didn't see successful women business owners or leaders in my real life. As a result, I followed suit and developed the view of myself that society told me to, that I needed to look pretty, not be too "extra," and always show deference to men because they had the responsibility to take care of us women and run the world.

As early as I can remember, I recall the idea of men having to be tough and "act like a man." Being at all feminine was the worst possible weakness. Strength meant no feelings, no sensitivity, and for God's sake, no crying. "Little bitch" or "pussy," both pejorative names for females, were the greatest insults a man could receive. The message women and girls received, and still receive today, is if the worst thing you can do to a man is compare him to a woman, being a woman must be pretty bad.

As girls, we saw long before anyone told us that a woman should never, ever emasculate a man. Never talk back to them, regardless of how they talk to you. Never, ever correct a man, even when he corrects you and is deadass wrong.

I got the teaching alright. But, here's the thing. No one ever sold me on *why*.

What would happen if men didn't feel superior to women, and women didn't reinforce that belief? My gut always told me that we'd not only survive, we'd all be better off for it.

Yet when every message you receive reinforces that male-dominant view of the world, it never enters your mind to challenge it. It would be like a kid refusing to go to school. It simply wasn't done. It was an unchangeable fact of life and arguing about it would get you nowhere.

Still, it never sat right with me. I saw no basis for thinking women weren't as smart or competent as men. In fact, women always seemed to get things done much quicker. I didn't see women as being more emotional than men, I just saw that the sexes differed in how they expressed their feelings and processed information.

I noticed a woman could become angry, scream, erupt in tears, then regroup, but an angry man could hurt you. Men had guns, where most women did not. Men would fight other men when unable to control their emotions, and the weakest of men would become physical with women and children as well.

Growing up, I learned a man's inability to maintain emotional control is far more lethal than a woman's.

I observed that women tended to analyze and gather evidence when making decisions. The men I observed tended to make up their minds right away and take immediate action. They didn't seem interested in considering alternative points of view or getting more information. They seemed confident, often overconfident, that they already knew everything they needed to know. To me, they could be impetuous to the point of danger. They made too many important decisions based on unproven assumptions.

Growing up, the primary difference I saw between the sexes was that men, more often than not, had bigger and stronger bodies. While those traits had tremendous value in the pre-industrial era, machines have equalized a lot of the physical differences between men and women. As long as women have opportunities to learn, they can do anything, and they don't have to adopt a male persona to do it.

It took many years of life, and the professor of my third-year trial strategy class, to see the differences between men and women as advantages I could use.

Until that class, I too, wore the Class A female lawyer uniform—navy skirt suit, white blouse, pearls, pantyhose, demure pumps and pulled back hair with minimal makeup. It's how society conditioned a woman living in a man's world to dress. But after examining why I believed what I believed and seeing little to no value in continuing to do things the way they've always been done, I decided to stop trying to overcompensate for the fact that I'm a woman and start embracing it.

My goal is to help girls and young women achieve these insights earlier than they occurred to me. Through speaking engagements, mentoring, and leadership in the professional world, I hope to teach these girls a little bit of what my law professor and Gloria Allred taught me, but earlier, so by the time they're adults, they're way ahead of the self-confidence learning curve. And boy do they need it.

When women and girls stand up, look their male opponents in the eye, and go toe-to-toe with them, their physical stature and limited voice put them at a disadvantage. Most women cannot match a man's voice in volume or resonance, but still they try, because they're afraid they won't be heard. When they do that, their voices often become shrill, making them sound even less credible. We have all seen Hillary Clinton and Elizabeth Warren fall into that trap.

A confident woman occupying her space is patient, but firm, and doesn't try to speak over everyone. She doesn't demure, either. I often use eye contact and hand signals to indicate I want to be heard, and when there's a break in the conversation, I take it. I do not, however, wait for an invitation—I take the in when it presents itself. The key is to not take the bait and argue over someone with a louder voice. Stand your ground and ensure your audience hears you. Don't let them move to another topic or close the conversation until you've spoken.

Importantly, if you are a woman who can hold attention, bring other women into the conversation. When speaking in a group of people with even one other woman in it, I always keep this in mind. When I see that other women have something to say but people aren't hearing them, I'll say something like, "Frank, you need to meet Sally. She'll blow you away. She's been working on this project for ten years and she's the real expert on this." Or, "Oh, if you're into psychology, you're going to want to know Carol. She just published her research in one of the journals of the American Psychological Association."

Any chance you get to bring up another woman or girl, take it. This also applies to men who see this dynamic. Every single one of us has seen a group skip over someone or wall them out of the conversation. We can all do more to include those people and their valuable contributions in the conversation. Those of us who can steer conversations need to model inclusive behaviors, so others will see us and do likewise. Bringing more women and girls into important discussions benefits us all. But first, they've got to feel confident enough to speak up.

Building Women's Confidence Starts Early, and We're Failing

One of my other female law partners, Rose Kasweck, judges the annual Tropicana Speech Contest at a local high school. For as long as she's done it, the top three finalists have been girls. As happy as that makes me, the minute I see the photos of the girls receiving their awards, I feel deflated. Each year, the all-girl finalists stand on stage to receive their awards hunched so far over, they look almost concave in the middle. Their smiles are meek. Their handshakes are weak. If you just walked in and saw these girls, you'd think someone had caught them sneaking into the movies without paying, and they could not be more ashamed of themselves.

Looking through the photos of those exceptional girls, I think back on all the graduations, honors, and awards ceremonies I attended over the years when my girls were in school. When the announcer called any boy's name, he'd start whooping and hollering and strutting across the stage, pumping his fists. And these were not necessarily the boys receiving high honors. It was apparent that almost all the boys seemed to possess a level of confidence missing in even the most accomplished girls. It was heartbreaking.

The girls, especially the ones receiving recognition for their exceptionalism, walked across the stage with sheepish smiles and heads tilted down. It's vexing to me that so many girls and women still don't receive their accolades with a straight back and a proud smile. Of course, I'm generalizing. I don't presume this pattern represents all boys or all girls. But there's enough of a disparity in how girls and boys respond to others honoring them that it deserves attention.

When girls do walk with confidence, and are eager to accept well-earned praise, society brands them as "arrogant," which has been my experience for much of my life. Although I knew from my upbringing arrogance was a negative trait, I almost never heard people accuse women of arrogance, only men. Women with aplomb tended to be labeled "snooty" or "stuck up." As an adult, I now see what the uninitiated regard in a woman as arrogance is, in fact, self-confidence. People just aren't used to seeing it in women. Now I love it when people call me arrogant. It means I'm shaking things up and making people uncomfortable. It means I'm using my space to help other women.

I shared my thoughts and concerns about the demeanor of these bright girl speech-winners with my law partner. I told her I wanted to do something to address it, so these girls would experience their successes as bolstering and encouraging, not, as it seemed, embarrassing. At the time, when I spoke to young girls, I already was telling them about the importance of posture and eye contact, but I realized it was time to turn it up a notch. From now on, I told my law partner, I would speak to them about using the unique advantages we have as women to occupy their space and command the attention they deserve.

One effective tool in teaching this to girls is to videotape them. There is something powerful about seeing yourself the way the world sees you. The girls and women I do this with note with surprise the effect of even the slightest change in posture. They see the power of maintaining eye contact with their audience: It brings their chin up, keeps their head straight, and gives them the appearance of a subject matter expert. Their physical size doesn't matter; by controlling their physicality, they create a larger, fuller, more powerful presence.

I think back to one of our former female marketing interns who has mastered this. Her back is always straight, she projects her voice, she speaks up in professional meetings, and she stands up for herself, even against people with more experience and power than she has. You better believe no one wants to tangle with her. She occupies all of her four foot eleven inches of space, and I do mean *all* of it.

Women do not remain in second-class status because of deficiencies in our appearance, height, strength, or voice. We remain there because we either choose to be there, or we don't know what to do to cause a shift. Women reinforce stereotypes of women by accepting there is no other way of being. Women perpetuate society's poor treatment of women by continuing to accept it without pushback. For most women, what holds us back is not so much our physical limitations; it's how we see ourselves. The image we project informs how others see and therefore treat us.

CHAPTER 2

Survival of the Fittest (That's You, Sister!)

We've all heard the phrase, "survival of the fittest." Not the biggest or the loudest, the *fittest*. The most agile. The ones who can roll with the punches and stay on their feet. Lucky for us, this is where women shine.

For as far back as I can remember as a child, I was fully aware of what my mother and I did not have. We exemplified the term "have nots." I swore to myself that the minute I could work, I was going to earn my own money and have all the things others had that I had gone without.

For the last two years of high school, I worked full-time at a law firm, handling the firm's books and processing real estate loan closings. It was a pretty serious, significant position. Although I was just thankful to have a job and my own money, I also found it comforting to receive praise for my work, which led to more complicated assignments, and greater responsibility. Every time I had free time, I asked to help a lawyer or paralegal so I could learn something new. One senior paralegal took an interest in me, taught me about legal research, and I soon took over managing the firm's law library. (This predates computers, so we're talking heavy ledger books and pocket parts.)

Even as a teenager, I saw that you have to speak up and risk failing if you want to move ahead in the world. Most people don't do that. Most people are content where they are or would rather stand around complaining than take the necessary steps to change their condition. Those are the people you can leap-frog over (more on that later).

By the time I graduated high school in 1985, at age 17, I was earning almost $20,000 a year and could not imagine how I'd ever spend that much money. I moved out of my mother's home right away and started living with two roommates. After a couple years of relishing my newfound independence, I started thinking about my future. Without a college degree, I knew my career options were limited.

I moved back home and enrolled in junior college, working part-time at a billboard company to afford my clothes and entertainment. My mother gave me the first $500 to pay my tuition, and I received academic scholarships for each semester after that. After two years, I earned my A.S. in Legal Assisting and started working as a litigation paralegal in a private law firm. That two-year degree served me well for many years. To this day, that degree remains my best educational investment for the money when considering potential lifetime earnings.

While I enjoyed being a paralegal, it was, by definition, a terminal position. A paralegal is a non-lawyer, no matter how much experience they have or how senior their status. It was time to return to school. I'd been out nine years, and it was going to be a challenge juggling all of my responsibilities, but I was ready. I was fortunate enough to be working for my husband, an attorney, which provided me with flexible hours to be with my daughter after school and still attend classes.

By any definition, mine was a miserable childhood. I would not wish it on my worst enemy. As a kid, I'd sworn that when I was an adult, I would become what I thought was a child psychologist so I could help children like me. My parents were very young, immature, and never spared me the unkind words they had for one another nor did they protect me from the adult level disagreements and accusations they made against one another. For as long as I can remember, I hated how it felt to have parents who despised each other. Surely there were professionals – counselors – who could help children in those situations and I knew I wanted to be one. Years later, my second husband thought I had a natural gift for listening to people and giving sound advice. With his encouragement and my continued desire to help children of divorce, I returned to school and completed my bachelor's and master's degrees in social work.

After graduating, I worked as a psychotherapist in an inpatient psychiatric hospital. After that, I counseled at-risk youth in the poorest county in our state. My plan was to work for a couple years under the supervision of a licensed clinical social worker, take the licensing exam, and become one myself. My goal was to have a private psychotherapy practice.

I worked with a multitude of clients whose lives were in shambles. It became harder and harder for me to listen and not take bold action. This led me to realize I'm a natural advocate, and that is how I can best help people who are hurting. Instead of counseling a victim of domestic violence, I wanted to go to court, get an injunction against her abuser, remove him from her home, and make sure she and her children were safe. It's hard to do that when you're only talking about feelings for an hour a week.

Ironically, during this same period of time I suddenly divorced, and was in danger of losing the safe, financially stable home I thought I had established for myself and my daughter. Using my degrees wasn't just a quest for personal fulfillment anymore. I needed to buy a house in the right area for schools, and I needed a job working for someone other than my husband. Take it from me, getting divorced from your employer sends you into a tailspin. When I meet women who work for their husbands but are not co-owners, it sends a chill down my spine. You have no idea what it means to have absolutely nothing until you lose your husband, your home, and your livelihood with one simple court filing.

So, the first thing I did was call all my contacts, which, though limited, were greater than I'd realized. Before long, the opportunity to manage a medium-sized law firm presented itself. I interviewed, got the job, bought a house, finalized the divorce, and relocated my daughter and me, all within one week. The divorce was inevitable – it takes two people to enter a marriage but only one to leave. There was no use crying about it then, I'd have plenty of time to cry later, when my and my daughter's lives had stabilized.

If I'm honest, my first inclination was to find another husband. I was an attractive 34-year-old woman. I desperately wanted more children. Because of my tumultuous upbringing, I craved a traditional family life. But my childhood and the sting of losing something I'd felt so secure in told me to invest in myself, not another husband. Oddly enough, I remarried the same man ten months later (that's another book in itself). I deeply loved him, and frankly, I was afraid I would fail on my own. Even if I had to marry the devil himself, I was not going to raise my daughter the way I'd grown up.

In time, things settled down, and after a year of managing the law firm, I again was unhappy with the direction of my career. Wanting to merge my legal background, counseling degrees, and desire to help women and children, I set my sights on becoming a family law mediator. My hope was to work with parents in mediation to not only resolve their outstanding legal issues but also support them in their coparenting. I taught mandated parenting classes as a clinical social worker and was ready to put what I'd learned into action with non-mandated clients. I hoped to stop parents from sharing too much with their children, badmouthing each other, using the child as a conduit for messaging, and give examples of how to better communicate and always put the interests of their children before themselves. I soon learned that was a lot to hope for in one three-hour session with two hostile strangers.

Getting divorced and losing the lifestyle I had raised my daughter in made me see just how easy it is to slide back into the position my mother was in as a single mom. After years of feeling financially secure, suddenly providing was all on me. Once again, I realized that to achieve long-term financial independence not tied to a romantic relationship, I'd need more education.

As far back as high school, I'd always been around lawyers. I held them in high esteem, considering them brilliant, cunning, and powerful. I'd been married to the smartest lawyer I'd ever met, and measured others by that standard. But after mediating a while and getting to know more attorneys, I realized they're just mortals. I also realized that most of them didn't seem any smarter than me.

Still, no one ever encouraged me to become an attorney. I grew up thinking that type of education was not for someone like me. Law school was for geniuses or children of privilege. But I reminded myself, my (re)marriage made me a person of privilege– I didn't have to work at all, really. I felt smart enough to be a lawyer. My grades were exceptional. I had a lot of great life and relevant work experience. Why not pursue law school?

Because my husband didn't support my going. That's why. In fact, he was hostile to it. He had lots of reasons, some rational, some irrational, but the bottom line was he didn't want me to go. If I set law school as my goal, it was going to be an uphill battle. Law school is hard enough without someone fighting you every step of the way. Still, nothing worth having is easy.

I squirreled away enough cash to open a separate checking account, for the sole purpose of establishing an account with the Law School Admissions Counsel (LSAC), the clearinghouse through which everyone applies to law school. I didn't want my husband to know I had applied because I figured if I didn't get in, that was one less fight we'd have to have. That didn't mean I wouldn't give it my best shot, though.

I bought every test guide and practice test I could get my hands on, and practiced taking them under timed conditions as often as I could sneak in three hours by myself. After about a month, my scores were good enough that, coupled with my grades, I was sure of admission. So I pulled the trigger and sent in my application. If I got in, I'd go. If not, I'd regroup.

But I felt conflicted. Becoming a lawyer wasn't like anything I'd attempted before. Was I cut out for the rigor, given my responsibilities to my husband, child, and home? Even graduate school was nowhere near as grueling or competitive as law school. I always made As, but in law school, everybody in the class has always been at the top of their class. Law school holds true to the curve. Somebody has to be in the middle and somebody has to be in the bottom half. I was determined it would not be me. I identify as an A student for a reason.

I worried that I might not enjoy practicing law, in the same way I felt unfulfilled as a paralegal, psychotherapist, mediator and manager. What if I didn't stick with it, or didn't even graduate? How much would I need to earn and how long would I need to work to make this a good financial decision?

It occurred to me, being a lawyer has greater value than earnings, which, at the time, I didn't really need. Being a lawyer affords an individual, particularly a woman, the flexibility to work from home, job share, and ability to hire help. If I ever did need to rely on my own earnings, and something always told me that eventually I would, a law degree afforded me countless options for career and financial autonomy. That being the case, even if I had to borrow money to gain my credential, it was a sound investment over the course of my expected professional career, which was another 25 to 30 years at that point. If I could manage the stress, of course. It's no coincidence that lawyers have reputations for substance abuse, depression, anxiety, and failed marriages.

I applied to only one law school, Florida State University, in the town where I lived. There were other law schools within a three-hour commute, but my daughter was just starting middle school, and living away from her was not an option I was willing to consider. I didn't want it that bad. In February 2005, FSU accepted me for fall admission. I was *thrilled*. I called my husband, told him I was going to law school at FSU, they'd already accepted me, and that I hoped he could get on board with my decision because it was happening. Thankfully, he did, because that day forever changed my life.

From graduate school and studying for the LSAT, I'd learned that I was going to have to become even more efficient if I was going to pull off law school with the kinds of grades I wanted without making my family suffer. Throughout law school, my heavy bookbag never left my side. If I was getting a pedicure, I was reading. If my child was getting tennis lessons, I was reading. While my husband was driving us to Disney World, I was reading. Wherever we went, on the way to dinner, the movies, the beach, I was reading.

Yet I never missed the important events in my daughter's life. I was there for the school luncheons, award ceremonies, birthday parties, and field trips. Because of my childhood, that was as big a priority to me as my education and career. I set those events in stone and found workarounds for everything else.

The traditional law school formula is to attend fall and spring classes, and work full-time during the summer with potential future employers. It's intended for you to try out different legal environments and see what's a good fit. I thought it best for my family and me that I get back to a normal routine as soon as possible, and opted to attend classes straight through, without taking the summer breaks. When I graduated, I hit the ground running in a career that has not stopped climbing since it began.

They say that once a woman experiences childbirth, she forgets all the suffering and pain. I think that's true for women in any challenge, not just giving birth. I almost never think back on the sacrifices I made to go to law school, or how insecure I felt about applying. Once I put that behind me, and my life really took off, I had so many other things to think of. But I should stop and give myself more credit for that. I'm proud of what I was able to do as a working mother. I think now of how intimidating and overwhelming the prospect of law school must have felt to the younger me, yet I found the fortitude and confidence to make that happen, with very little encouragement. I should take more time to relish in that accomplishment.

Yet, this is what we women do every day of our lives—far more than we thought we could, and far better than we could have imagined, for the simple reason that we have to. We are the last to opt-out of responsibility. It's in our DNA to adapt and excel. But it sure would be easier without so many outdated ideas and attitudes standing in our way.

Had I accepted conventional wisdom and stayed in my lane, I'd still be financially dependent on someone who is now an ex-husband. As a paralegal, my earnings were above-average, but I had virtually no upward mobility. Many paralegals' high earnings are tied to a specific attorney or firm, and when those attorneys retire, die, or sell their practices, those paralegals are either out of a job entirely or looking at a huge pay cut. It's not so different from the position many women find themselves in as wives. If the husband dies, leaves, or becomes disabled, they're looking at an abrupt reduction in standard of living through no fault of their own. That's a precarious situation to be in. Plan for it now.

Don't Climb, Leapfrog

Climbing the corporate ladder is not the best way to get where you want to be. It's grueling drudgery, it's outdated, and it disadvantages women because it fails to address or accommodate our unique challenges. It's designed by and for men, which makes sense, because they got there first. They got to set the rules. That doesn't mean you have to follow them, though.

Take the private law firm model as an example, but this could be a bank, insurance agency, large corporation, government office, or roofing contractor. You come in as a law clerk while still in law school. If you're lucky enough to get a job offer, you start as a junior associate. A few years later, you advance to senior associate, spend a few years there, then hit the big time as a junior partner. If things go well, you move up to senior partner/profit-sharing partner. If your drinking or other stress-induced destructive habits haven't caught up with you yet, you may continue on to shareholder, do that for another 15 years, and retire with a decent nest egg and myriad health problems.

But consider how that might work for a woman interested in having children or maintaining a traditional role in a traditional marriage. Around the same time that she's looking at becoming a senior associate or junior partner, she starts thinking of beginning a family. For no reason other than biology, that can take her out of the workforce or limit her participation in it, resulting in significant losses in earnings and career advancements.

Yes, I realize that many employers offer parity in maternal and paternal leave, but it will be a long time before men and women have parity in parenting responsibilities for newborns. That also doesn't consider the consequences of carrying a child. Women have many doctor's appointments during a healthy pregnancy. If she's high-risk, as women in the workforce tend to be, because they postpone pregnancy or experience high stress, she may have additional doctor's visits or have to stay on bedrest. All of which makes her less available for travel, meetings, networking, socializing, and all of the other activities that promote career development.

When the children arrive, more often than not it's the mother who stays home with the sick child or attends doctor's visits and school functions. It's the mother planning the birthday parties, vacations, playdates, and putting together school costumes and projects. Most women can't or don't want to spend six hours golfing on a Saturday. or sitting in a cigar smoke-filled office on a Monday night playing poker, just so they can have a say in running a company. That is a large reason many professional women take a competitive backseat and don't engage with their male peers. The costs of that non-engagement are immeasurable over the course of their careers.

There isn't enough time for women to pay dues the old-fashioned way. If a woman wants to have children, it's even more pressing to find the shortcuts. When I say "shortcut," I don't mean half-ass it. I mean look for the ins. Have a playbook to be sure, but know that a lot of the time it isn't going to work. That's when you find another way to move the ball down the field. That is when you leapfrog.

I'll give you an example. When I decided to complete my college degree, at the time, I knew I wanted to have a private practice as a psychiatric counselor. I assumed that meant becoming a Ph.D., an expensive process that can take up to seven years. One day in my work as a paralegal, I happened to interview a witness in a malpractice case who was a professor at the Florida State University College of Social Work. Through her, I learned I could reach my goal in three years, if I completed a bachelor's, then a master's of social work–a terminal degree I could use to become a licensed clinical social worker. That decision alone saved me not only extensive tuition costs, but years of upward mobility in my career. All because I asked an expert a few questions. I thought I had a plan, but knew I didn't know everything, and that there was probably more than one way to reach my goal. By looking around at the resources available to me, and having the gumption to take advantage of them, I leapfrogged over four years of education that wouldn't have helped me as much as they would have cost me by not earning and advancing those four years once I'd achieved my ultimate goal of having a clinical counseling practice.

Similarly, I used everything I had both during law school and once I started practicing. Fourteen years of experience as a paralegal was a decided advantage but not as much as living with and working for an almost obsessive attorney who was incapable of leaving it at the office. I listened to, and learned from, that brilliant maniac almost 24 hours a day for many years. Because of my proximity to him, I gained exposure to depositions, hearings, mediations, and trials typically reserved only for people with law degrees. It would have taken me at least five years as a practicing attorney to learn what he taught me simply by being in his orbit.

That invaluable up-close-and-personal training I got from my husband provided the basis for my next leapfrog career opportunity during my last year of law school. My husband ran into a local attorney he often litigated against who knew my work. My husband mentioned I was about to graduate law school. The attorney was planning to retire and needed someone to take over his caseload and eventually buy his shares. This led to a series of conversations and me ultimately receiving an offer for a once-in-a-lifetime opportunity. On April 18, 2008, I was sworn in as an attorney at 11:30 a.m. and became a named partner in a 30-year-old, established plaintiff's personal injury law firm at 4:00 p.m. the same day.

One good thing about not having as many opportunities to choose from is that women can appreciate how rare they are. We can't assume another is coming right behind the one in front of us, so before we pass on it because we're too busy, scared, or inexperienced, we need to consider the likelihood of having another shot.

Women need to become comfortable with risk. We can do that by conducting meaningful risk/benefit analyses and looking at challenges through as objective a lens as possible. We do it by seeing ourselves succeeding and by starting ventures with the knowledge that we will not fail.

Too many times we look at our lives and decide they're fine. And any disruption would be harmful to us, our family, and our peace. But I'd like women to challenge that thinking. Is it true, or are we using complacency as an excuse to not reach the next level?

By encouraging women to leapfrog, I'm saying take calculated risks, use everything you've got, and bypass traditional methods of paying your dues. You don't have time to do it the old way. It's not realistic to break into anything the conventional way, because the people who got there first, a.k.a men, already occupy the field. You may be leapfrogging over your competition. Maybe you're leapfrogging over societal limitations unfairly imposed on you because of your gender, age, orientation, education, or lineage. Look for innovative ways to release yourself from those constraints.

Buy Back Your Time

Extra money can help in a more practical way, especially for women who perform the bulk of domestic chores in a household. I'm a fan of "buying back your time." At a recent conference of women trial lawyers, I got to hear a presentation from a woman who has mastered this. The presenter was a personal injury trial lawyer from Atlanta, married to another attorney and pregnant with her third child, probably in her mid-30s. After a few grueling, dues-paying years at a traditional southern law firm, she realized that at that rate, she'd never get where she wanted to be. So she took a calculated risk. Instead of trying to bust through the glass ceiling at someone else's law firm, she left, started her own firm, and took her old firm's clients with her. At the time, she was married and her first child was still an infant.

She saved $2,000 and started her own law firm, working from home. She contacted every colleague and law school classmate she knew who might get personal injury cases. She asked for referrals and offered to co-counsel on languishing personal injury cases they'd mistakenly agreed to take on despite having no actual practical experience. Within a few months, she'd put away $40,000, which was enough to rent an actual office and employ one person part-time.

Unlike a lot of people starting their own businesses, she didn't focus her efforts on practicing her craft. She focused most of her time on growing her business and networking her contacts. She could always hire another lawyer or more staff to handle additional legal work, but if there was no work to do, it didn't matter how great a lawyer she was, her business would fail. By staying laser-focused on growing her business, she added two attorneys and more staff in a few short years.

While her business was booming, so was her personal life. She had two more children and moved into a larger home. She put the same organizational skills she'd used to start her firm to use managing her personal life. At first, she had a person who picked up her child from school and stayed in their home until she and her husband returned from work. She started asking the caregiver to pick up groceries on the way home. That led to delegating other tasks. Eventually, she sat down and listed everything she and her husband did on a regular basis that someone else could do. Then she used that list to buy back their time.

Now, they have a person who works for them, 3:30 p.m. to 8:30 p.m., Monday through Friday. This person picks up their children from school, goes grocery shopping, runs errands, prepares dinner, cleans up afterwards, and packs lunches for the next day. This way, when the attorney and her husband get home, they get to enjoy each other, have a nice meal, and take a walk or play with their children instead of feeling hurried and exhausted.

When the attorney recognized she didn't have to do every single thing a mother and a wife typically do, she and her husband noticed a dramatic improvement in the quality of their relationship, and they had more patience with their children. They didn't enjoy cooking every night or cleaning up afterwards. They certainly didn't enjoy feeling exhausted and short with their kids and each other. To get her time back during a time of professional growth, she knew that to make much more money, she needed to spend just a little more money.

People who aren't growing a business, or can't afford a personal assistant also can recognize the benefit to buying back their time. The fewer their responsibilities, the less thinly they have to spread themselves, and the higher their quality of life. The more time they buy back from mundane, routine obligations, the more time they have to spend on meaningful endeavors they enjoy.

It seems obvious, but why don't more women do this? It's often because we don't stop long enough to assess our situation and the people available to help us. You can't just hire anyone. It takes time to find someone, vet them, train them, and build trust with them. You have to view it at as a long-term investment in yourself and your family.

To buy back our time, women also need to let go of the stigma around taking a nontraditional approach to being a wife and mother. In the early 1990s, when Hillary Clinton's book *It Takes a Village* came out, conservatives lost their minds because the book suggested raising children is a communal responsibility, rather than solely that of the child's parents. It was a ridiculous overreaction. It does take a village to raise our children. It takes parents, grandparents, teachers, neighbors, mentors, healthcare providers, and yes, sometimes nannies and housekeepers. And that's fine. We're not living in our grandmother's or mother's worlds. It's time we act like it, and make choices that work for us. It takes a village to raise a child, just like it takes a village to live through each day. Find some people you trust, in the same situation as you are. Help take care of each other. Pool resources by redistributing work, like *I can drive our kids from school to practice. Can someone go to Publix and get these things for me and drop them off on Monday?* They use Venmo, Zelle, or PayPal to send money to each other. They see their time as a commodity and they optimize technology to facilitate sharing resources.

Many women think they can't afford this kind of help. That's not true. There are people starting services on a membership model, where subscribers pay a fixed amount per month for a certain number of hours from a personal assistant. If they don't use the hours, they roll over. If they need more hours, there is an additional fee per hour.

Still another option for women who need to buy back their time but cannot justify spending it on these types of services is to form a co-op where people trade the services they provide for the services they need. One person may be a great cook and offer meals in exchange for another person picking up her children from school and taking them to soccer practice. It's all about being innovative and assessing the value of the resources you already have.

It's still uncommon, but I'm seeing women come together and link resources like never before. They're tired of prioritizing things they don't value, like excessive meetings, bureaucracy, and male-oriented networking, and giving short shrift to the things that matter to them, like time with their families, volunteering, and personal development.

I recently spoke with a lawyer from a group of four women who left other firms to begin their own practice where they pool resources to have a better quality of life. They have low overhead, because they've all mastered technology. They help each other with their children and personal errands. Although they each have their own separate practice, they're available to work together on a case-by-case basis. They have the resources of a bigger firm without all the overhead and management problems.

Aside from time and money, there's another resource women often fail to optimize—contacts. If you're homegrown with generations of contacts in your city or town, leverage that. You can also make money from social media. People with no training at all can become social media influencers with the ability to earn income or gain goods and services. If you have a large number of followers, leverage them by offering to promote small businesses.

I'm always amazed at the cases and opportunities that come my way because of some crazy connection I had with someone. It can be as simple as having given someone's grandmother a ride home 20 years ago or as memorable as being vomited on during a flight (more on that later!). But beware—networking can turn into a waste of time if it's not done intentionally.

When life abruptly slowed down during the initial COVID-19 quarantine, I had a sudden increase in free time. I started wondering what the hell I'd normally be doing but for the quarantine. I reviewed my calendar, beginning in January. The things I had made time for shocked me.

My calendar was full of lunch meetings and drinks with people who only wanted something from me. They weren't offering anything of equal or greater value in exchange for my time. It ranged from board meetings to non-profit requests for money to mentoring sessions with college students. All of those things have value, but when I saw how much of my time this consumed, and how little I got in return, I decided I had to change. No wonder I was always frazzled and felt like I didn't have time to do the things I wanted to do. My time was scattered all over the place but I wasn't making any demonstrable difference with it. I wasn't being intentional enough with my time.

Set Your Mission

My law partner, Jimmy Fasig, emphasizes the importance of having a mission and setting goals that are congruent with it. Your mission, he explains, is something you can say in just a few words. It's your purpose. It's what you're passionate about. A mission statement informs and directs your goals and intentions. It needs to be simple. This is mine: *My mission is to promote and protect women and girls.*

I arrived at that by trying to focus on where my passion lies. I looked back over how I'd been spending my time, and realized I didn't make a lot of measurable progress. I'd served on boards, hosted events, and written a lot of checks, but it never manifested the results I hoped for. I'm sympathetic to many causes, including homelessness, hunger, and mental health, but sometimes when you try to do too much to help too many diverse interests, you can spread yourself too thin to be effective. I realized I needed to drill down on what really matters to me.

I looked at every appointment on my calendar, identified those that had nothing to do with my mission, and crossed them out. I looked at the time and money I was spending at galas and fundraisers, again under the premise of marketing my law firm or helping a nonprofit. For many years, event organizers would tell me they were giving me an award or honor, only to ask me to donate $5,000 to be the title sponsor and finance the entire event. Now, when I consider making charitable contributions personally or from the firm, I consider whether it gets us business or directly helps our clients or women and girls. If not, I say no thank you.

To do that, you have to watch your ego and understand the psychology of sales. It is not your obligation to support someone simply because they've decided this is the time that they want to pursue their life's goal of running for office or starting a business or non-profit. It is fine if you want to, but it can sometimes feel like you're as invested as they are in their dream's success. There's a good reason for that – it's a tried-and-true sales tactic. That's why you're called "host" or "chair" at events and presented with awards at big galas – in hopes of a donation or contribution commensurate with your ego.

Once I streamlined and prioritized my interests, like writing this book, speaking to women's groups, investing in women-owned businesses, and mentoring women and girls, my calendar made more sense. My ten, five, and one-year goals came into focus and the path towards achieving them clearer. My one-year goals turned into monthly goals which eventually distilled into to-do lists. And there is no greater joy than checking something off a damn to-do list. This all was possible because I chose a mission informed by my passion—building up women and girls.

Find the Ins

My first paralegal position was in Montgomery, Alabama in 1991. I only lived and worked there six months, but it formed an indelible memory. Paralegals back then wore "power suits" with broad lapels and thick shoulder pads. They seemed like mini-lawyers, almost like lawyer impersonators. Having your own office as a paralegal back then was a huge deal, but that meant working in the basement, way outside the flow of what was happening in the belly of the firm. As a result, we'd receive projects without understanding the bigger picture of what the case was about. I'd think, *how can I summarize a deposition in a meaningful way if I don't know what's important in the case?* It didn't stimulate me. I couldn't stand not being involved.

So, I looked for opportunities– the ins. The senior associates and junior partners, all men, seemed to be the ones doing the heavy lifting. If I impressed the senior partners, they'd feel comfortable with the junior partners giving me opportunities. In one case, the plaintiff had been leaning against a truck when its boom contacted overhead power lines, which were supposed to be inactive, electrocuting and killing him on-the-spot. I offered to summarize a technical deposition of the opposing expert to assist the senior partner in preparing for an upcoming trial. It was clear the lawyer didn't think I'd be able to understand the subject matter, probably because I was a girl. Still, he gave me a shot.

What the senior partner didn't know was I'd worked for a billboard company in junior college, and was familiar with the exact type of crane involved in the case. I still had contacts from that job, and was able to call people in the industry who could answer my questions. With their help, I was able to take technical testimony and explain it in a way six jurors with average eighth-grade educations could understand. In a memo to the other partners, the senior partner praised me, saying, "I took the expert's deposition and I don't even understand his testimony as well as Dana does." That was the moment I realized it wasn't terribly hard to impress these men. They had such low expectations for me.

That led the other partners to value my input and include me in case preparation and development meetings. They gave me greater responsibility because I took a chance and asked for something considered above my ability.

Because I wasn't content to stay in my downstairs office, waiting for empty assignments, and instead read the room, looked for ins, and believed in myself, I made a big impression in a short time. When my husband's company transferred us to Tallahassee, one of the founding partners in Montgomery personally called his Tallahassee attorney contacts to help me find a job. I didn't know a soul in Tallahassee when I moved there, but had a job within a week.

Reading the room involves looking for unmet needs and becoming invaluable by filling them. It builds your power, which is important— you can't do anything without some power. It's out there. It's up to you to find it.

In any organization, there is a power structure. Whether it's a marriage, business, or church, there's a power structure. Find out who the decisionmakers are and what they respond to. The ones with the power are not always the loudest or most visible. Find out how they use their power. Are they collaborative decisionmakers? Are they surrounded by yes men? Are they open to feedback?

Always look at who the players are. Who's got the power, what do they prioritize, what do they value? Look for what they're missing, see what you can add, and that's your in. That's how you get there, by learning how to read the room.

There's Less Competition at the Top

My work now is far easier than it was when I was starting out, running around the country deposing doctors and trying medical malpractice cases. My primary focus now is growing and marketing our firm. When I first started practicing, I had a lot to overcome. I live in a man's world. People wondered how I got my partnership opportunity. Many, I'm sure, thought I slept with someone. Strangers assumed my male law partners must be my brother, father, or husband. I felt so many people itching for me to do a huge career faceplant. That was plenty of motivation for me to make sure that didn't happen.

For the first several years I practiced, while I developed and improved as an attorney, the firm was stagnant. Some years were more lucrative than others, but we weren't growing or distinguishing ourselves from all the other personal injury attorneys. We provided good service to our clients, but rarely was it exceptional, life-changing service. My younger law partner and I thought we could outperform our competition if we focused on extreme client service and making our attorneys accessible and relatable. Those differences changed our entire practice, and our lives.

In any business, your competitors will reach a state of complacency. They'll get to where they're earning a fine living and enjoying an above-average quality of life. They're going to Europe every year, just not on a private plane. Bureaucracy or inaction often stifle creativity and innovation in their firms. Employees tend to stay two or three years then move on. It's a comfortable treadmill many business leaders are content to log 30 years on and retire from. Beyond that treadmill is where the opportunities are for the rest of us. We can sweep in and scoop up everything those people have left on the table.

Disruption is one of the most powerful tools women have. No one's looking for us at the higher levels. No one sees us coming. They see us as something they have to tolerate in the modern workplace but rarely much of a real threat. We are either background or ornamentation. When I started practicing law and plastered my face all over town, we started hearing about it from our competition. They said things like, "How are we going to compete without a pretty blonde in our ads? That's not fair."

Potential clients weren't accustomed to seeing ads with women trial lawyers, either. Trial lawyers tend to be the peacocks of lawyers—kind of showy. Well, so am I. I embraced that through my femininity. But the power of being a female trial lawyer is greater than that. I learned that when people are hurt, when they feel vulnerable, they often prefer to talk to a woman, an angle I optimize in our advertising. As a woman, I have unique advantages that distinguish me from my competitors. And I use every single one of them.

Our firm started growing, and we enjoyed greater and greater success. Because I had surpassed my competitors' level of success and was taking their clients, they started to show me genuine respect. I'd proven I could do something they couldn't.

Once you bust through that level where most people get comfortable, it's like driving around late at night. There aren't a whole lot of people on the roads. It's not hard to stand out. If you have any personality at all, it will be easier yet. If enough women take me up on this, and start taking risks and embracing what makes them different, we will soon have a new pandemic: one of female empowerment.

We found that in personal injury law, staying small gave us more competitors. Growing our firm beyond that mid-level where most other people unpack and put down roots resulted in fewer competitors. There is money to be made if you're not too complacent, fixed, or stuck to go after it. Find what you do better than anyone else. Find what the market wants and isn't getting, and provide that missing piece. Think from your customer's perspective. Give them what they're asking for, not what you want them to have.

Make it About More Than Money

Money is important. We need it to live, it can make life easier, and you can do a lot of good giving it away. I love money. However, I found that despite a childhood of longing for it, after a certain point, money was no longer my primary motivator.

For me, doing more motivates me, helping and reaching more people. Professionally, I want to help more hurt people. There are a lot of people hurting in the world who feel powerless to change anything about their lives. When they come to our firm and trust us with their case, our job is not just getting them a check. We help them sort through their finances and learn how to make their money work for them. We put them in touch with a mentor, counselor, coach, or advisor. We help them plan their new businesses. We link them to resources they can trust. I've seen clients come out of multi-generational poverty because they were able to take a horrible tragedy and use it to change their lives for the better. I've seen clients become financially independent for the first time in their lives. I've seen them go out into the world, knowing they'll no longer be victims. So many of these clients are women.

That's why I want you all to come at least as far as I have, and go further. When women finally get something awesome, they want to share it with other women.

CHAPTER 3

Always a Bride, Never a Bridesmaid

've been married and divorced *four* times. "Always a bride, never a bridesmaid" is my tongue-in-cheek way of dealing with the subject when it comes up. The truth is, I don't think it's very funny. Not at all. But it is what it is. In my fifties, I like to think I've learned some lessons from each of them.

But, seriously…no one has *ever* asked me to be in their wedding.

Raised with Unrealistic Expectations

I grew up during the second wave of feminism in the 1970s, when women in the movement saw their mothers' and grandmothers' marriages as traps, almost like social life sentences.

They wanted no part of it. They rejected traditional marriage and family because it felt restrictive and limiting.

I wasn't raised around women who held this point of view. The women I knew pitied this new generation of women. They saw feminism not as empowering, but as a threat to their way of life. These women looked forward to spending most of their efforts raising children, caring for their husbands, and making a home. And they seemed to be in a big hurry to do it. They felt the feminist movement signaled the end of the traditional home and would eliminate alimony and child support, should their husband/bread winner not stick around.

As a budding adolescent, I suspected the feminists were having a blast. They were raising hell all over the news and television talk shows, and while men seemed to be losing their minds over it, the feminists rocked on. I admired their bravery. They either didn't care what society thought, or didn't show it if they did.

Although I admired the feminists, I didn't aspire to be one. As a child, I'd spent enough time alone to never want to be alone as an adult, no matter how glamorous Marlo Thomas and Mary Tyler Moore made being a single and successful modern woman seem. Growing up with a divorced mother and an absent father, a "real family" was something I craved. I spent considerable time fantasizing about how it would look and feel to be married to a reliable husband and provider, where I could play a supporting role taking care of our home and children.

Without a lot of successful, independent women as role models, it never occurred to me to prioritize *my* success. From what I could tell, my husband's success would determine mine. I knew I'd need the best husband I could find if I was ever going to have a beautiful home with two and a half perfect children and a dog named Dave.

It would take me almost 30 years of combined marriage experience to learn that simply was not true.

I Did What I Knew

Most women get married the way I did the first time, assuming they'll be in a supportive role, believing marriage is something you have to check off the list to start your grown-up life. This model often comes with considerable pressure, because all your girlfriends are getting married around the same time. When I wasn't married right out of high school, people started praying for me at church. When I *finally* got married just after turning 22, they'd already written me off as hopeless.

I never doubted that as a wife I would be secondary to my husband. They use the term "support staff" in offices, and that's how I view women in traditional marriages. You're there to support the higher earner. Under that model, a married woman is thinking:

> *I sure hope I picked a good one, because all my eggs are in his basket.*
>
> *That career of his better take off.*
>
> *He better be one mature, reliable dude. A provider. If he can't do it himself, I'll come behind and build him up, whatever it takes.*
>
> *I did not take myself off the market for this man to fail.*

My mother often told me, "never be reliant on a man," citing my father as an example for why not. It sounded great in theory, but I'd seen my mother struggle financially without a partner my entire childhood. It didn't look so great to me. I thought she could've used some help.

All around me, I saw women competing against each other to snag the best provider possible. It looked like landing a good husband was the Holy Grail. He's the finish line. You get him, and you're done. After that, all you have to do is make babies and create a lovely home. And the first time I married, despite my mother's warnings, I did just that.

My first marriage felt like a trap almost immediately. The day before my wedding, I could take my money and buy whatever I wanted. Suddenly, I had to check with my husband first. If I decided to return to college to complete my degree, I had to get his consent. Any form of personal enrichment came second to my obligations and expectations as a wife, then a mother. My husband, child, home, and work all came before anything I wanted for myself. Yet it didn't seem that way for my husband whose needs and wants we prioritized. Because he far out-earned me, I simply accepted this. I thought that was the essence of the marriage contract.

Marriage felt constraining. Like I was giving more than I was getting in exchange. I felt relegated to Class B status, permanently cast in a supporting role. If there was ever any leftover time or money, maybe I could take up a hobby. Yet unhappy as I was, "being divorced" seemed far worse than staying in an unfulfilling marriage.

My first marriage lasted a little over five years. Most people who knew us when we met didn't predict we'd make it that long. He was twice my age when we married, older than both of my parents, and I was still a girl trying to figure out how to be a woman. We were in different developmental stages and never fully understood one another. Our marriage produced a bright, bold, beautiful daughter we are both so very proud of. And 26 years later, I am grateful I can call my first husband one of my dear friends.

Addiction Confused with Love: Marriages #2 and # 3

I entered my first marriage with the conditioned belief that marrying a stable man, having children, and building a family is all a woman needs to be happy. When I entered my second and third marriages, I still held that belief, but thought it would be different, better, if I was married to a husband I was hopelessly in love with. That, I told myself, is the *real* Holy

Grail. Turns out, what I thought was love, was addiction, and like most addictions, it almost killed me.

My second and third marriages were to the same man. We were married about six years, divorced ten months, and remarried for eleven more years. Years ago, I heard a comedian liken the decision to remarry someone to taking a big swig from a carton of milk, spewing it all over the place, screaming, "Oh my God, that's sour!" then putting it back in the fridge thinking it'll be better tomorrow.

In these relationships, average isn't normal average, it is fucking fantastic. For me, most of the relationship felt like the best days of my life. But the other part was full-on Armageddon, end of days, horrific. The things two people who "love each other too much" can say and do to one another are downright sinful.

It seems impossible a relationship that volatile lasted twenty years, but we were both convinced the other, despite their flaws, was "the" special one. We could rationalize anything. Oversee any deficiency. One such rationalization was that I was subservient to my husband. I felt, as many women do, that this was a natural position to take because women still typically have less power in their relationships, primarily due to lower earning power.

The person with the power in any relationship is always the person willing to leave it. Usually, in a marriage that power is tied to money. Many women can't afford to leave without suffering a major decrease in their standard of living, and men, of course, know that. Therefore, women tend to accommodate men's wants and errant behaviors, instead of addressing them, or outright leaving.

Part of what makes it easy for women to fall into this trap of accommodation is the belief that our partner's success is our own. If they fail, we fail, so we do what we must to build up and support them. When I was caught up in a love addiction, I found it even easier. I thought, *If I'm gonna have to build up a man, it may as well be the one I can't seem to live without.*

Conflating intense attraction with love can derail a man, just like it can a woman. We've all seen successful men marry women who are not their intellectual equals. Or guys who are patient, kind, and forgiving, yet always seem to take up with women who constantly criticize and complain about them, often in public. No one is immune to the feeling of having finally found your soulmate, the unique individual you are sure the universe created just for you. I fell prey to that twice. But when I stepped back and looked at the relationship objectively, and actually wrote down the pros and cons, I realized there was no reasonable basis for the two of us to be together. Doing something about it, though, was much harder.

Too Good to Be True: Marriage #4

I met my last husband the day I decided to get divorced from my second/third husband. Two months earlier, my husband had filed for divorce. He'd done it in anger and we were treading water to see if things might calm down between us. One Thursday afternoon, sitting in my office, I had an epiphany—my marriage was over. It was simply never going to be okay. It was never going to settle down. It was never going to be easy. It didn't need more time, more effort, more anything. We'd left everything on the field, and it was *over*.

The very day I made up my mind to walk away from 20 years with a man I felt deep love for, I met a man who seemed too good to be true.

And he was.

Because I made him that way.

Once again, we had incredible chemistry. And, once again, I set about becoming his perfect mate, taking up all manner of activities I had little to no genuine interest in. I saw in him everything missing in my previous marriages. Remember, I'm a trial lawyer, spin is my game. The problem is that I've mastered using that skill against myself. In my fourth marriage, I used every red flag the universe sent me to create a beautiful, floor-length cape I wore with hubris. Because I wanted it, I convinced myself I'd found my soulmate. It was some of my best work.

I entered that relationship committed to it being my last. I looked for and found all the evidence I needed to feel confident going into yet another marriage, just a little over a year after ending the last one. I ignored every sign that said he and I were about as compatible as water and oil. At our core, we had fundamental differences with few similar values, beliefs, or interests. But I was having a fantastic time. I was with someone I was intensely attracted to, and ignored anything that didn't reinforce my decision to choose him.

After a mutually disappointing two years, the marriage ended, as it should have. I spent over a year in therapy, drilling down on the lessons I needed to learn, fighting the depression I'd developed over yet another failed marriage. I had to face the truth about myself: As much as I considered myself a progressive person, a feminist, a modern woman, I was scared to not be married. I had been married, to somebody, for 28 years. Over half my life. Not being married was as foreign to me as waking up with a third eye, and in many ways, less desirable. People are kind to freaks, but not when they've chosen it.

Being married was familiar, if uncomfortable. Yet when I decided to start dating again, that was my goal. I looked for appropriate prospective husbands. Not the love of my life – I wasn't that naïve anymore - just the most appropriate person. I still felt I needed to be married to be seen as a serious person, given my profession. In my quest to achieve homeostasis, I once again found myself changing to accommodate whatever my male interest wanted or needed. Accommodation seemed inevitable, so I looked for the man who'd require the least amount of it from me.

After several months, I realized if I didn't change my entire orientation to relationships, I was destined to repeat my mistakes. I needed to have some fun. To take some pressure off dating, and just enjoy the company of someone interesting. To stay in the moment and not view every date as a potential husband. It finally occurred to me that maybe marriage wasn't the best romantic framework for me.

The silver lining is I'm doing just fine. As trite as it sounds, I feel like I'm living my best life. I travel whenever I want, with whomever I want. I grow my business without worrying how my success might harm my marriage. I prioritize my other relationships. I enjoy watching my daughter find her way in the world as a young adult, without the same artificial, culturally-imposed limitations I felt. And when I date, I stay in the moment. I enjoy being with a person without projecting us into the future and fantasizing over what our couple-style will be. I laugh a lot, and I have *fun*.

My former husbands, each of them wonderful in their own way, have moved on to enjoy relationships with women who are infinitely better suited for them than I ever was. This pleases me. That's how I know I've learned the lesson I'm supposed to get from these experiences: when you truly love someone, you want them to be happy. Even if it's not with you.

I'm Fine Just the Way I Am

A deep examination of my marriages revealed one common experience among them: eventual rage. I see now how it developed. I contorted myself to be what I believed these men wanted. But they didn't recognize or appreciate it or contort themselves to be what I wanted. So, I complained and got shut down. I didn't feel heard, so I became resentful. Resentment turned into anger and when anger festers over a long enough time, it turns to rage. Not a full-blown, boiling-over rage. I'm talking about a rage that simmers. It's always there in the background, permeating every relationship experience.

Unchecked anger and resentment is what causes a couple to go nuclear. It's what causes us to assume the worst about one another and jump to the wrong conclusions. It's what makes us stop giving one another the benefit of the doubt. It's what leads partners to use each other's deepest secrets and vulnerabilities in a fight. That's when the fissures form. It doesn't take much of a hit after that for the entire thing to crumble.

In relationships with rage in the background, partners stop sharing their lives and confiding in one another. They don't want to show any weakness, for fear their partner will bring it up in a conflict. That is an unsustainable dynamic. No one should try to sustain it. If a relationship gets to that point, it's abuse. Get help, get out, or both.

Your Future Is Not in Your Past

When I think rationally and ignore societal expectations, I know I made the right decision to leave my marriages. As humiliating as it is to admit that I was married and divorced four times by the age of 50, I don't have the slightest doubt that it was necessary to have the life I want.

Still, when I'm by myself a while and don't have a romantic interest, I think about how great it would be to have a partner. Someone to share all the things I love with. Someone to show affection to. Someone who gets me. Sure, I get forlorn over past relationships and ruminate over what I wish I'd done differently. It's natural to want to go back and try again with past loves. I get that. I really do. But past relationships ended for a reason. Trust that.

When I brood over past relationships, my rational brain eventually kicks in and says, "No, honey. You're rewriting history. You're forgetting how bad it was because you are lonely right now." Rational brain is correct. It's like having a baby. The minute that slimy sucker pops out and they plop her on your chest, you forgot about the 18 hours of labor. You forget about the third-degree perineal tears, sitting on a donut for two weeks, and the first horrifying bowel movement after giving birth to that monster, (few of which I actually experienced—this is hyperbole). All you see when you look in those big little eyes is love.

Same with old romances. You forget the gritty horror of past relationships when you're lonely. Everyone wants to love and be loved. It's nothing to be ashamed of. And it gets more frustrating looking for love the older you get. Most people are married or turned off to it. It's slim pickins to be sure. Just remember past relationships are in the past because that's where they belong: that milk is not going to turn fresh tomorrow. So, don't take the bait. Turn on Netflix. Read a book. Listen to a podcast. And for the love of all things holy, do *not* hit send!

Marriage Isn't the Only Option

As much as I would like a great relationship with an incredible person, I now see marriage as one of many forms of relationship available to me. It has obvious benefits, but a lot of them I don't need, like financial security, a parent for my child, or health insurance.

Beyond that, the benefits of marriage I do need and want, like companionship and sex, are not exclusive to marital relationships. Religious beliefs don't inform my decisions about relationships. I'm not interested in having more children or finding a parent for my adult daughter.

Admittedly, it helps not needing someone financially. I appreciate that many people, even more nowadays, need the extra income a partner brings. Yet younger generations seem to understand better than my generation, marriage is not the only form a romantic relationship can take. I frequently meet Millennials and Generation Z-ers who live together, buy homes together, raise animals together, and have children together without being married, or who go many years before making it "official."

Modern women see how enriching their lives can be without an exclusive mate, married or otherwise. Some women enjoy having light relationships with several people. Many have fulfilling, celibate lives. Remember, women have only given themselves permission to aspire to something other than a support role in a traditional family for a short while. We're just now exploring our alternatives.

As obvious as a self-determined life may sound to younger women, it's foreign to many women of the Baby Boomer generation. There are those who broke off into the hippie subculture, but there are many in whom society instilled values of spousal duty and self-sacrifice These are women whose parents suffered through the Great Depression. They put God, country, and men first, because those things were what kept them safe. To do otherwise would have been disrespectful and self-defeating.

I recall a saddening statement a therapist shared with me about his observations of his many female clients over the age of 65. He remarked on the sheer number of women who sit on his couch lamenting their decisions to spend their entire lives putting their husbands and families first. He has helped countless women in that age group process deep despair and regret for not taking their shot. For not leaving after their kids went off to college, got married, and had their own kids, or after their husbands retired. Worse, as is typical of women's suffering, not only did they feel they'd missed out on the best years of their lives, they were sitting in a shrink's office, paying him by the hour to blame themselves for it. As we say in the South, *bless their sweet hearts.*

While women are almost never in a superior or even equal position in a marriage, even today, I am not necessarily negative on marriage. I don't believe my marriages were unsustainable because marriage sucks. What I see now is that the old model of marriage doesn't promote an egalitarian power structure. For any woman who insists on equal power, it's flawed.

Marriage doesn't need to be kicked to the curb; it just needs an update, like any other operating system. Sure, there will still be women who sign up for marriage 1.0, but those women are harder to come by, and they're not gonna just give you their credit card and put you on auto-renewal.

The old model of marriage is losing traction for many reasons. but the largest is that husbands today cannot provide at the level husbands have in the past. This means a woman's income isn't optional, it's essential, which in turn causes a redistribution of power within the relationship. Power follows money, even in the home.

The more women earn, the less deference they will show to men. Much of the deference men have enjoyed is owed to their earning power, not their gender. Logic dictates that when earnings equalize, so must power. That is why so many men and women vigorously oppose equal pay. They say it upsets the "natural order." Well, that's grade A baloney. Women head more households now than ever before. Never have they needed equal pay for equal work more than they do now. And never has there been more momentum behind their fight for it. This is our time.

You are Your Own Worst Spin Doctor

We've talked about why self-respecting women stay in bad relationships, now let's explore *how* they do it. I can tell you stories about women who keep their husbands under electronic surveillance at all times. Some install voice-activated recorders in their husbands' vehicles. Others hide nanny cams throughout their homes and husband's offices. Still others hire private investigators. All to prove to themselves something they already know: there is no trust in their relationship.

To those women, I ask you to remember, all the evidence in the world doesn't matter if you're unwilling to leave. Until you're ready to consider leaving, stop looking for evidence in support of a case you're never going to make. You're better off not rubbing your own nose in it.

If you even feel the urge to spy on your partner, you already have all the information you need. You have a trust problem in your marriage. Either you're projecting your own insecurity onto him or he's lying to you, directly or by omission. Spend your energy working on trust, not catching him in the act of something. Work on why you feel he's being dishonest with you, and how long you're willing to live like that. Trust your gut, not his ridiculous explanations.

Instead of working on the problems in their marriage or finding the courage to leave, these women create their own reality to justify tolerating their partner's behavior. We've all heard the excuses.

The Children: *I will not break up my children's home. I won't put them through a divorce. They're too young. They're too old. I will not raise them in poverty. I will be home for my children, and I can't do that if I leave.*

Money: *If I leave, I will lose my lifestyle. I can't enter or re-enter the job market or college at my age. We can't afford two separate homes. I can't earn enough to make up for losing his income.*

Status: *I will not be a "divorced woman." My children will not come from a broken home. I'm not moving out of this neighborhood. My children are not going to public school. I'm not going to work.*

In every circumstance the message she's twisting herself in knots to avoid hearing is the same inner knowing: *I don't trust him. I'm not safe with him.*

Women in these situations know their partners are not going to treat them fairly or with respect. They also know they can't behave in the same abusive way that their partner does, because he actually may leave her. So, they look for ways to mitigate the situation. To make it as un-bad as it can be. That's where these women live their lives. In the spin zone.

He's not as bad as Sally's husband.
I do have a nice standard of living.
He'll calm down when he gets older.
What man treats his stepchildren as well as he does?

It's bad, but I did get to start my own gallery, go to grad school, and not have to work outside the home.

We all make mistakes in our relationships, but we don't have to suck at fixing them. It starts with being honest. Maybe this relationship is nothing more than me falling for a guy who blew my skirt up but isn't really marriage material. Or maybe this person seems like a suitable mate, but I'm ignoring the fact that there is no real connection. Whatever fiction we tell ourselves, we feel stuck, so we stay. We take whatever emotional scraps are available to us and build a life around them. We try to convince ourselves he's the one, when in our heart, we know it's just not supposed to be this hard.

A Constant State of Compromise

Ever notice how a relationship can devolve over time? You don't notice any abrupt changes, but when you reflect over how things used to be and how they are now, you find yourself wondering, *how in the hell did we get here?*

One commonality among my past relationships was feeling I lived in a constant state of compromise. A constant state of accommodating my partners' unique sensibilities so there would be peace in the home. I put my wants and needs last if anything caused unease with them. I noticed myself dreading telling them about my plans, be it meeting my girlfriends, attending an event, or travelling for work. I knew they would be grumpy about my being gone, or jealous, or whatever their insecurities led them to feel. I had to hide things from them or tell half-truths because I knew they'd feel insecure about me being around people outside their presence. If mental gymnastics were an Olympic sport, I'd have taken gold. Anything that made them uncomfortable, I either withheld from them or didn't do. Because I knew how they'd react, instead of telling them in advance, I'd spring my decision to do something at the last minute to avoid living with a sulking man for two weeks.

I traded one big blow-up fight for a cloud that hung over my home for weeks at a time.

When I was single, I would've told my partner about my plans and my enthusiasm for them. I wouldn't have thought twice about doing anything I enjoyed. But as a coupled person, I'd always had partners who were upset anytime I exercised autonomy. They took it as rejection and it prompted jealousy and baseless accusations. So, I started withholding the truth, or some of the truth, or outright lying. I walked on eggshells, careful to avoid all of their triggers. In this way, those relationships turned me into a dishonest person. I didn't like myself as much. I felt guilty, so I acted guilty. I'd get caught in half-truths, which made the lack of trust between us even worse. In trying to placate my partners by limiting my autonomy, I changed my own character. Over time, I turned into someone I didn't respect.

At that point, I had two options: exercise my agency, or give up what mattered most to me to keep the peace. I felt trapped, like an accomplice in my own imprisonment. I became angry, because I felt ashamed about what used to bring me joy. What's wrong with hanging out with my friends or taking a weekend trip with my law partners? Giving up what I loved just to keep the peace created tremendous personal dissonance, which lead to anxiety, depression, and substance abuse. All because the romantic partners I chose were uncomfortable not being in complete control.

Sound familiar?

If it does, know you're not alone. It happens to more people than you think. It sneaks up on you. I didn't realize how much compromising I'd done until I couldn't recognize myself anymore. That's when the resentment started. Anger and rage were just around the corner from there.

At some point, you have to face the fact that you don't have an infinite amount of time to live the life you want. It's not going to start when the kids go to college. It's not waiting to start until retirement. It starts when you decide to have the life you want. Lots of marriages survive a woman's transformation into the person they've always wanted to be, and grow stronger for it. It's an opportunity for both partners to make their relationship a real priority and grow together. If they'll take it. Your relationship is probably stronger than you think. I'm certain you are. Your partner will survive if you stand up for yourself and what you want. It will not kill him. But unchecked resentment can kill even the most passionate relationship.

Other times this transformation in a woman ends a marriage. Even when you both want it and know it's the right decision, divorce *sucks*. But sometimes it's the only path to the life you deserve. And yes, you will survive it. You will come back stronger. If you're brave enough to commit to living your best and fullest life, with or without your partner, you've already got everything you need to ensure your success. You have courage and optimism. With those traits, you can do anything.

Divorce Isn't Failure, It's Growth

When women are unhappy in a marriage, they often say, *I deserve a better life.* Or, *I don't want to expose my children to this. I don't want them to have this life.* A lot of women arrive at that conclusion and stop there. They don't take the next step and get divorced. For those of you who do find the courage to make the necessary changes to live the lives you want, I applaud you. It's an act of bravery, not failure, and you should be celebrated.

It's scary to think of leaving a relationship. It feels like being the only person who can't do this one thing that everyone else seems to have mastered. Many women are more afraid of being alone than staying with an abuser, or someone negative who constantly brings them down. In the world today, being a woman is a low-status position. Being a divorced woman can appear to diminish a woman's status even further, because divorced women often perceive themselves as "damaged goods."

I want to challenge women who have experienced divorce[1] to see themselves not as damaged, but empowered. Look what we had the bravery and wisdom to do that so many others did not.

The fear of failing in marriage is so pervasive among women that even the most successful among us lose ourselves holding onto a relationship we know will never work. In the HBO documentary, *Jane Fonda in Five Acts*, Fonda discusses how she reinvented herself to become what the men in her life needed, from her father to her last husband, Ted Turner. She was in her fifties when she was with Turner and felt her acting career was over. She was well cared for as his wife and would never need to work again. She loved him deeply. Yet after ten years, she left.

About leaving Turner, Fonda says, "if I stayed, I was never going to become who I'm meant to be as a whole person, as a really authentic person." She was 62 years old the last time she divorced. She is now 82 years old, her career is on fire, and she's back to getting arrested for her political activism. Seems like a pretty authentic life to me.

Walking away from or accepting the loss of a relationship before it's too late to have the life you want takes incredible resolve, and an abiding belief that your future will be better than your past.

After it Ends: Now What?

You will receive what you expect to receive in this world; it's up to you to decide what that is. After my speaking engagements, I tend to have five or six women approach me and one common refrain I hear is they feel their lives are over after a divorce. Like they've taken their shot, it didn't work out, and now can only throw themselves into raising their children, caring for their parents, or volunteerism. Ironic, isn't it, how once women

---

[1] (see how I didn't label us as "divorced people?")

finally have time to focus on their own wants and needs, we still focus on others?

We never do get comfortable putting ourselves first, do we? When airlines instruct passengers to put oxygen masks on themselves before assisting their children, they never use men to demonstrate that point. Men have always known their duty above all else is to survive. They know they can't provide and protect if they're dead.

Women have an instinct to meet others' needs first and put themselves last. Imagine how great the world would be if men had even a sliver of the humility most women possess. The whole world needs a correction. Women need to learn to believe in themselves about as much as men need to learn to put others first. We all have some growing to do.

If your attempts at being a good wife, mother, and home-maker don't succeed, it's natural to feel like a failure. Your brain tends to imagine others' marriages are perfect, and they're living the dream you could never have. It's normal to feel that way. It's not rational, though.

It's natural to want to be in a couple. To have someone to share your day with. It's normal to feel lonely. To want someone to touch you. To want someone to leave notes for you and text you because they're thinking of you. You can have that if you want it. It can come in many forms, from lifelong marriage, to years-long affairs, to one-offs. Be open to finding the romantic platform that works best for you, wherever you are in your life right now. Every date doesn't have to be your next lifelong mate. Stay in the moment and enjoy learning about and experiencing new people. And trust me, some of the best stories come from dating misadventures.

On Dating, Generally...

I'm no expert on dating, but I've done a lot of it, and observed years of dating behavior in others. I studied relationship dynamics in undergrad and graduate school, but never practiced couple's therapy for any significant length of time. My musings on this are a combination of my education, lifelong observations, and personal experience. So, take them for what they are: good, solid advice.

First, make this your mantra, *I will think logically and rationally.* If you do this, it will be hard for people to hurt your feelings, and you'll have the bravery to take risks, resulting in a better shot at happiness.

Second, trust your instincts. Logic, rational thought, and intuition can co-exist. Logic and rational thought ensure your decision-making is free of emotion. Intuition applies your inner wisdom to your decision-making.

This is not the same as being cynical or incredulous. It's not waiting for the other shoe to drop, thinking nothing great can really happen. That's negative, self-defeating programming, based on past experiences or societal conditioning. By being humble and recognizing limits, even when you don't want to see them, you open yourself to receiving signals from the universe.

Cultivate Impenetrable Self-Esteem

So much of our self-defeating programming derives from an insufficiency of genuine self-love.

The feeling that I didn't have breeding held me back for much of my life. No matter what I accomplished, I always felt I wasn't worthy of being included in certain groups because I was poor, came from a "broken home," didn't have a dad, and didn't go to college the right way. It kept me from taking risks and experiencing the resulting pay-offs. It was why I chose the men I did.

I didn't feel like I was good enough for those awesome guys who encourage you. The ones always telling people about something incredible their wives are doing, or going on about how they don't deserve her, and can't imagine why she chose them. I fantasized about being married to someone like that, and always thought, *those men are not available to me. I'm not good enough to have someone like that.* I envisioned their parents learning of my background and thinking, *why did he choose her when he could have done so much better?*

Three days before I turned 40, walking across the stage to receive my law degree with high honors, Order of the Coif, no less, the feeling that I was good enough *finally* hit me. The sense that I can have anything anyone else has. That there was never anything wrong with me to begin with. I hope the women and girls reading this book and coming to see me speak don't wait until they're 40 years old to truly believe this about themselves.

In graduate school, I learned that people obtain their self-esteem in one of two ways: Through competency, by doing things well and receiving recognition for it, or by having a great childhood, growing up with people who made you feel loved, secure, and empowered. What little self-esteem I did have as a girl and young woman I'm certain derived from competency. I had above-average grades, mostly acceptable behavior, and an inordinate amount of good luck. Still, nothing can substitute for a childhood foundation of security and support, something I lacked.

But there is a path to self-esteem for people who didn't win the childhood lottery and don't feel particularly competent. You can cultivate self-esteem through rational thought and listening to your intuition, to the point where these senses lead you to create a different experience of life. Right now, today, commit to knowing you are good enough to be anyone's friend or mate because you are a good human being who cares about the world and the people living in it. If someone makes you feel like you're not good enough, because you don't have an ivy-league degree or the right family connections, be thankful for that information. It's something you need to know. Because that relationship, my dear, is not good enough for *you.*

Dealing with Rejection

Finally, can we talk about the sting of rejection? Because if you put yourself out there in the dating world, it's going to happen. Rejection is a universal experience.

I've had people I really dig send signals they dig me too, then ghost me. Crickets. I've mulled over every conversation I've had with those people, pored over every text and email we've exchanged, looking for clues as to why they've rejected me. It feels blindsiding and hurtful.

This is when I call on my rational, logical brain. I think of the potential mates who were really into me, who I tried to like, but couldn't find enough of a connection to build on. It could be for any reason, but the punchline was I decided he wasn't the one for me. Now, would I want his entire view of himself to plummet because *I* didn't feel a connection to *him*? Would I want to see him curled up in a ball, crying, not getting out of bed for days because he wasn't my cup of tea? Of course not. I'd want him to understand sometimes things just don't work out. It's nothing personal, and I'm sure the right person is out there for him. I wouldn't want him thinking he was worthless and no one would ever love him, so why would I let someone's rejection make me feel that way? It's just not rational.

On Dating in Mid-Life

As little as five years ago, if you would have told me I would be happily divorced and dating again at age 52, I would've told you to stop hallucinating. Dating in my early 50s took some getting used to, but now I love it. Now that I've gotten a sense of humor about it, that is.

This is unchartered territory for a lot of us. I often find myself in the company of men and women within ten years of my age who are newly single or in the process of divorcing. They're ending long-term marriages and their children are pretty much grown and launched. They're trying to date again. No one, and I mean no one, knows what they're doing.

Some revert back to 1970s-1980s high school dating behaviors. Things like telling a mutual friend to tell someone that they like them, and see if they like them back. Or sending you an email or friend request, which is the 2020 equivalent of passing the note, "Do you like me? Check one: Yes ___ or No ___"

Others go straight-up insta-dating. They swipe left and right, have virtual hook-ups, the whole multidimensional relationship experience. As an advertising lawyer, my face is plastered all over buses, billboards, and television. I'm not putting my mug on a dating sight. I already get more attention than I can handle. In my case, what I need is help sorting through it. I tried hiring an agency that finds matches. The first "match" they generated was no more suited for me than my three ex-husbands, so I figured I could do just as well on my own.

I've found people in their 50s and 60s are looking for more than companionship in finding a mate. They consider how long they're going to work, what their financial needs will be in retirement, and how to protect their assets. Although I no longer have to consider a potential mate's earnings, that doesn't mean they don't consider mine.

Like anyone who experiences divorce, I questioned my judgment as I re-entered dating. In the year it took me to regain my footing, I felt insecure and uncertain. By nature, I'm a trusting and optimistic person, but suddenly, I have more than my heart to protect. I have my own money and need it to work for me far into the future. I determined to never need a relationship for financial security, which made me almost paranoid about the intentions of potential suitors. Whenever I meet a new, too-good-to-be-real person, I see them setting up an elaborate six-to-nine-month con operation to break my heart, humiliate me, and put me in the poorhouse.

Dating in your 50s and 60s is challenging. It isn't like when you were in college and your dating objective was to find an attractive mate who could be the best protector, provider, and future father of your children. Now you're going to dinner with people who are Medicare eligible or within five years of it. Sure, you're both still interested in sex, but no one wants to see the other person walking around naked.

And the dating pool is shallow. The available people were either burned by divorce or languished for years in a lifeless marriage. Many have had lots of short, shallow relationships and never grew up, or have just lost their saintly wives to the ravages of disease. It's pretty rough out there.

I know I don't speak for everyone, but dating in your third quarter isn't very romantic. At times it feels more like a salvage operation. Statistically, you have a small chance of finding *the* one. And that's okay. Find the one with whom you can coexist. They usually turn into "the one" over time.

That's the great thing about dating later in life. With no pressure to have children and build financial security together, you can choose your mate for other reasons, like mutual respect, compatibility, and companionship. Plus, you have all your life experience to pull from. You know what you like. You know what you don't like. You don't need someone at your side 24 hours a day to feel secure. You can have your own interests outside of the relationship in a way that enhances it, and not at the expense of it.

Beware the Share

There are things I understand now that I'm older that were inconceivable to me in my 20s and 30s. For example, I can be a couple, but without marriage or even cohabitation. I have my life, he has his, we share parts of our lives together, but we can maintain separate homes or live in different cities.

Mature dating also includes not knowing everything about the other person's past or keeping up with what they're doing all the time. Young couples often find this unimaginable. Their desire is to have such a strong connection, it's like they're enmeshed. But what real benefit comes from oversharing with a partner? I cannot recall one time when knowing my partner's history, especially with regard to other women, benefited me in any way. Yet it's almost instinctive to over-share.

Retain a little mystery. You are not the same person you were when you were with your former lover, and the circumstances are certainly different. The lessons from that relationship have limited value, so don't give them more space or attention than they deserve.

Before you cough up every hurt and disappointment from your past, ask yourself what you expect to get for it. Sympathy? Them to label you as damaged or bitter? Them to rescue you? And how long do you want them to see you that way? Is that where you want to reside in a relationship? As a powerless, angry victim in need of rescue? An unloved woman mad at the world? Watch what you share first if you don't want to have that image for the rest of the relationship. Never start in a downward power position. It's too easy to get stuck there.

On Dating and Disappointment

Be ready to face disappointment. It's a fact of life. Women tend to look for the best in others while seeing the worst in themselves. Men disappoint us, and we can't help but wonder why. We're dealing with a fast-changing world where gender roles blend more every day. Why can't men be more agile? It's not survival of the most rigid; it's survival of the fittest.

Dating in my 50s has taught me, men are simple operating systems. What intimidated them when they were young intimidates them now. What they strove for as young men, they still aspire to as they enter their senior years: success, stability, and respect.

But now, these men aren't getting pushback from just younger women (who some try, ridiculously, to date), but also broads their own age. The women in their own generation are evolving at a fast pace, and no longer make building up a man their top priority. It's easy to see why these men feel confused and overwhelmed in the modern dating arena. Things aren't working like they used to. Nothing makes sense from their perspective. Women have changed quicker than men have been able to adapt. This is how all meaningful growth occurs. It has to hurt a little.

Many men have deep insecurities. I imagine it's from the endless pressure they feel to take care of everything and everyone, and appear to have it all while doing so. When they appear successful, people treat them better, with reverence. That's important to men. That is why they gravitate toward the prettiest, shiniest, and brightest, even if they don't really want it. They convince themselves they want it because other people judge them by whether or not they have it. A good woman may make an insecure man happy, but she's not worth as much to him if his friends don't want to fuck her.

When you're old enough to understand this dynamic, it's disappointing. You thought a relationship would be deeper. You thought it would be more intellectual. You thought it would be more intimate, like maybe someone would see you for the wonder you are after all these years. You can't believe it's this basic. But it often is. That is why I encourage women not to make their romantic relationships the most important thing in their lives. That's too much pressure for your partner, and it's just not fair to burden them with your ultimate happiness. That's your responsibility.

How to Have a Rational Relationship

I have a very close relationship with my law partner, Jimmy Fasig. He's an odd duck, cut from a different cloth. He can control his thoughts and emotions through meditation and sheer will. He inspires me every day to be my best self and my life has been deeply enriched by his presence in it.

As a joke, we sometimes refer to our relationship as a marriage, but without the fun stuff. To achieve success in our business requires all the features of a successful marriage.

I've said many times, I will not remarry or cohabitate until I find a relationship like the one I have with Jimmy—a relationship where my success is as important to him as his own. Where I match his enthusiasm and we both look for ways to actualize the other's dreams. Where we each see the benefit the other brings to the relationship, and express gratitude for one another's efforts. Where I know I'm free to take risks and push myself, because he has my back 100 percent of the time. I'm fortunate to have that in a business partner. We've translated our interpersonal success into commercial success and it has enabled us to help thousands of injured people. When I envision the support of a romantic partner, I realize I must accept nothing less than I receive from my law partner, or I will never be at my best.

To assess whether a relationship fits this bill, I search deep within myself, and consider my core values—my mission. My life's passion. I envision my ideal life, congruent with these values, and reverse engineer it, starting with where I want to be and breaking down how to get there.

When doing this with a prospective partner, I ask myself a few key questions.

Can I grow with this person? Is he only interested in this version of Dana, or can he handle my evolution?

I have long believed that women marry and divorce the same man, but men marry and divorce two very different women. Change in women is inevitable, but not all men are able to accommodate it.

Is he trustworthy?

This isn't just about not lying. Being truthful should be assumed, not aspirational. This is about whether I can be vulnerable with this person. Can they maintain a confidence? Can I trust them to support me when I need it?

Do we share common values and beliefs?

By the time I entered middle age, my values and beliefs were pretty fixed. Everyone likes to spar now and then, but that's not the same as having a knockdown, drag out fight every time the news comes on. Now I look for diversity of opinion outside of my romantic relationships, but for my home, I want someone I can get along with.

Are our lifestyles compatible?

If he's slowing down professionally, and I'm ramping up, I'm honest with myself about how long we can sustain divergent lifestyles. If there's a large disparity in earnings and assets, I have to consider how I'll handle that. Will I have to curtail my enjoyment because my partner doesn't have the same resources or interests?

And finally, the big one: *How does he fight?*

It's important to find out how someone handles conflict early on. Do they sulk, hurl insults, throw your vulnerabilities in your face? Do they give you the silent treatment and completely shut down, refusing to work through or even acknowledge problems? Worse, do they gaslight you? Try to convince you that you're crazy, a bad person, then tell you all the significant people in your life agree with them? Does it feel like they're trying to break your spirit?

If you're ever in a situation where you feel this way, run, don't walk, *run* in the opposite direction from this person. That is psychological abuse, and no one deserves it.

Asking yourself a few key questions before committing to a person takes a lot of the fun out of a new relationship, but please trust me on this: getting divorced is a *lot* less fun. As you read this, many couples are enduring painful separations because they didn't ask these questions earlier. Take the time early on to look at your potential partner with your eyes wide open.

CHAPTER 4

If You Can Conceive It, You Can Be It

What limits women the most is not trying, not going for it. Because I guarantee you, whatever you commit to, you will accomplish. How many times have you considered something another woman started and said, "Well, she failed; that didn't work out for her."? Not many. Yet I bet you know lots of stories about women who achieved financial or career success against great odds. I can tell you about scores of women who never tried, but I can't tell you about many who tried and failed. Whatever your goal is, make a commitment to just do it.

For me, my life-changing commitment was my decision to go to law school, despite the disruption it would cause in my family's life, and the lack of support my husband showed for it. Once I made that commitment, not only would it happen, it would be a successful endeavor. Not once did I consider dropping out, taking a break, doing less than exceptional work, or not passing the bar exam. Those were not options. Once I adopted that mindset, there was nothing left but to do it. That's how women are—once we stop listening to everyone telling us we can't do something and make up our minds to do it, magic happens.

Be Selfish: Make Time for *You*

Women receive so many limiting messages. For instance, "you don't have time." In many ways it's validating to "not have time" because it acknowledges the mountains of responsibility women have. Most of us work outside the home, while bearing the overwhelming majority of responsibility for the home, yard, children, extended family, healthcare, shopping, family event planning, and logistics. We hear friends, family, and even ourselves, say "you just cannot take on one more thing, you're barely keeping your head above water as it is." It's easy to believe you don't have time for things that matter to *you*. But when your partner, kids, co-workers, friends, or parents need something from you, like magic, you make the time—for them. That's twisted.

Making time for yourself isn't selfish. It's maintaining a vital operating system. For optimum performance and safety of your car, you change your oil and maintain your brakes and tires. Failing to maintain your physical and mental health is no different, except if you run a car into the ground you can buy a new one. You only get one body and brain.

By always doing for others, we end up always seeking their validation. When it doesn't come, we can become resentful and cynical. But when we make time for ourselves, we receive internal validation from our own accomplishments and willingness to care for ourselves. By always putting others first, we rob ourselves of our most joyful lives.

So, use that magic to make some time for yourself.

Beware Seeing Yourself the Way Others Want You To

When I was a young woman, I worked at a regional accounting firm with partners who were all white, male, and middle-aged. One afternoon, in the breakroom, some of the partners engaged me in conversation. To this day I cannot recall the topic, but I remember none of them expecting my response. One partner reacted to my contribution with the exact words, "My God, you are *brazen.*"

I didn't know what brazen meant, but I could tell he wasn't trying to flatter me. So, I looked it up: *Brazen, adjective. Bold and without shame.* No doubt, he meant not just to insult me but to put me in my place, to remind me *he* would determine what was acceptable female conduct, not me. A huge smile crossed my face. I thought, *brazen, huh? I like it.*

That was one of the first times I realized how unprepared men are for women to challenge them in any way. It doesn't happen often, so they haven't had much experience with it. I made that man so uncomfortable with my irreverence that he couldn't let it pass, he had to remark on it and try to make me feel ashamed. I'd thought I was an insignificant support staff member, yet I got under that big man's skin just by speaking my mind.

Yet how many young women in 1988 would have decided to let that exchange embolden them? What about in 2020? Still not enough. Too many women would have allowed that exchange to shut them down. Too many would have left that conversation feeling defeated, reluctant to ever speak up again. When that happens, those women don't get to make decisions, and the decision-makers don't consider their interests. As Elizabeth Warren says, "If you don't have a seat at the table, you're probably on the menu."

I don't know why I chose to walk away from that experience feeling emboldened, but I'm glad I did. Seeing myself as brazen changed the trajectory of my entire life.

Watch What You Accept as Gospel

Often the factor that limits us the most is our own thinking, our preconceived beliefs about what is and is not possible for us. Most of the time, they don't come from us.

When I was a therapist, the psychiatric hospital where I worked admitted a patient because he was suicidal. I remember he described himself as "just a 50-year-old, beat-down queer." He personified sadness. After a few sessions, we learned that as a boy, an older man had sexually abused him for many years. The abuser told him he was queer, he wanted the abuse, people would make fun of him if they found out, that his parents wouldn't believe him, and his homosexuality would disgust them.

We also learned that the patient had never had sex with a man, other than his abuser, and had no attraction to them at all. In fact, he much preferred women. He'd never attempted a relationship with a woman because he believed he was gay. His therapist ultimately suggested to him that maybe he wasn't gay. No one had ever given him permission to think of himself in any other way. For over 35 years, the patient experienced chronic depression, at least in part because he identified as gay when it never felt true to him. All because someone told him something about himself and he accepted it as an immutable truth.

When I first became a lawyer, I took everything my ex-husband, the trial lawyer, said as gospel. If he worked a case a certain way, I believed that was the only way to work a case. I looked at the business decisions he made in operating his law firm as the best way to run any law firm. It took me a while to realize he didn't know everything. He gave me a wonderful foundation, to be sure, but that's all it was. A foundation on which to build.

Because I received an amazing partnership opportunity right out of law school, the attorneys I used to be co-counsel with as a paralegal, now opposed me as an attorney. It was inevitable there would be professional jealousy and doubt. One day, after a contentious mediation, I received an email from one of the opposing defense lawyers, addressed to me, and all the other lawyers and staff on his team. I read the first sentence, which began, "Dana sure is pretty but she's not very smart." The moment I realized the author had not intended to send it to me I stopped reading. When the sender noticed his error, he contacted me, and started apologizing. I cut him off, saying, "That's not necessary. I only read the first sentence. Your opinion of me is none of my business."

It took incredible discipline and self-esteem to not read the rest of that email. I was tempted. But I knew I'd be reading the words of a frustrated man not at his finest hour, and frankly, it was none of my business. To read more would have been to eavesdrop on his thought process. But think how damaging it could have been to my psyche had I read further. Worse, what if I'd internalized his view of me when, in reality, he was just venting because I was thwarting him on a case? No good could come from that.

One day, it dawned on me. The people who were most uncomfortable with me were the ones I had outperformed. I'd only been a lawyer four or five years and I'd out earned them, I'd served more clients (whom I actually care about), I'd grown a three-man law firm into a 10-lawyer, multi-million dollar law firm with multiple offices. I'd created scores of well-paying jobs and a working environment where people flourished. And I did all that coming from nothing, with no advantages or contacts, without my husband's encouragement, and in the face of active haters. Who the hell were *they*?

And you know what happened? People started treating me congruent with how I felt. They started to see me the way I saw myself. I started receiving requests to serve on important committees and offers for leadership roles in my community. People sought my opinion. They asked me to help them achieve their goals. And all that had changed was what I believed about myself. Remember, the only way to change someone else's behavior is to change your own and watch their reaction. *You* get to determine the truth about your life. Because no one knows it better than you.

Redefine Your Expectations

Getting yourself and other women to buy into the mindset that women are competent, equal human beings, not second-class citizens, is monumental. It's upsetting we're not further along. It owes in large part to how women value themselves.

I saw this with striking clarity when a super-fan from Valdosta, Georgia called me. From her accent and manner of speaking, I discerned she was an older Southern woman. She said my commercial had prompted her to reach out. In the specific ad she mentioned, we'd revealed a scam where insurance companies show up right after a car crash, and convince victims to sign away all of their rights for a nominal settlement, before they can appreciate the seriousness of their injuries. The woman told me that within an hour of her car accident, an insurance adjuster had approached her, offering $500 to settle her claim. Because of our commercial, she knew not to take it and to seek legal representation instead. She said she liked how tough I was, and that's why she wanted me to represent her. Those are the kinds of calls I live for.

But as she kept talking, problems arose. She kept coming back to how "tough" I was and how much she liked that. But what she meant was, w*e aren't used to seeing tough women like you, and I like it. It's different.* It's cool that she likes it. What I don't like is that it's different. A tough woman shouldn't be an anomaly in the twenty-first century.

Second, she said, "I don't know if that's your brother or your husband in that commercial with you, but I like him, too. He looks like he's as tough as you are," referring to my law partner, Jimmy Fasig. This revealed her assumption that I could not have achieved my success on my own. I must be the sister or wife of the man in the commercial. I bet she never wondered if he got to where he was in life on my coattails.

As much as I wanted to receive her intended praise, I felt deflated. What little progress women have seemingly made since I was a young girl arguing with my mother about the need for states to ratify the Equal Rights Amendment!

Keep in mind that we are in the American rural South. Most small businesses here are still family-owned, and men dominate decision-making in homes, businesses, and communities. Of course that woman would be surprised to encounter a woman like me! She's not used to seeing it.

I chose not to take offense at her reaction, and instead tried to nudge her expectations for what a woman can become in a little different direction. My mission is to create a world in which no one is surprised to see a self-made woman heading up a multi-million-dollar company. For that to happen, people have to expect to see it.

No Windups: Check Your Language

A common theme I hear when speaking to women is that they are uncomfortable speaking in groups or offering original ideas. They're almost apologetic about taking up space, as if their contributions don't deserve as much consideration. Women often start sentences by apologizing, "I'm sorry, but I disagree with that...," or offer a long windup, so when they finally get around to sharing their thoughts, their listeners are lost in parentheticals. Don't make people burn calories trying to figure out what you're trying to say. If it's important enough to say, fucking say it.

This reluctance to speak out comes from two things: a society that devalues and dismisses women's opinions, and the resulting low self-esteem in women who grow up with that messaging experience. But where is the truth in the message that women's contributions aren't as important as men's? I challenge you to find it. It's not a truth, but a choice women make about our value. I'm asking us to choose better.

That starts with language. Instead of saying, "I'm sorry, but I disagree with you," try saying, "I get what you're saying, but consider this…", or "I'm trying to see this from your perspective and it sounds like ____ is important to you. I'd like to talk about _____ because ____." Speak from a position of power. Instead of saying, "I'm sorry I was late. My kids were being crazy," just say, "I appreciate your patience. Let's get started." You can be polite and firm. Those things are not mutually exclusive.

How many times have you heard a discussion or debate where a woman says, "You're exactly wrong, and here's why." When I've said it to men, not like I'm mad, just firm in my position, their jaws drop. It results in a change in their behavior, because they know I'm not going to just roll over. They've got to either drill down on their position and engage in meaningful debate, or abandon the issue. Over time, I've learned men often get their way because no one challenges them. Their way isn't better; people just haven't questioned it.

Part of checking your language is calling out mansplaining when you see it. Men have no compunction correcting women, even when they are deadass wrong. Men will attempt to mansplain a concept to a woman who has already researched, written, and published books on it, and is now lecturing about it to her peers. And women just take it. We roll our eyes and shake our heads. I'm asking you to stop doing that.

When someone mansplains to you, stop and correct him. But don't offer a quick dismissal, or they'll write you off as an over-sensitive female. Make it painful. Make it tedious. Tell them how when they explained the concept, they assumed you don't know as much as they do about it, and they're wrong. Give specific examples. Tell them how it makes you feel, and how it effects your regard for them. Do whatever it takes to make their treatment of you so painful it doesn't happen again.

Understand that the disrespect and marginalization women experience is because women tolerate it. I have literally had a grown man tell me, an adult woman, that "there are some things a woman should never say to a man." Yes, in the twenty-first century, there are still men, and women, walking around believing that nonsense. It's time to stop tolerating it. Men are not superior to women. It is not your job to maintain their ego.

One way to check if you're tolerating this, is to ask yourself, when someone critiques a contribution you've made, if a man doing the same thing would've received the same criticism. If the answer is no, then don't give it another thought. It's not your job to deliver bad news wrapped in sunshine and flowers simply because you're a woman. If gender isn't relevant, don't make it relevant, or allow anyone else to either.

Learn to Lead

One of the biggest obstacles to women's success is learning how to lead. It's a numbers problem. Women just haven't had many leadership opportunities outside their home and volunteer work. Those of us who do find ourselves in leadership roles got there in most cases by watching and emulating those who came before us, mostly men. When that's the only leadership model, that's the one we tend to perpetuate. We've all heard horror stories about bosses who were super aggressive and couldn't build consensus. Or weak and ineffective bosses, who failed to get their team to produce. Or manipulative bosses, who pitted people against one another. But like everything else in our lives, we have the power to change these stories.

Do not compare yourself to male leaders. Don't let anyone else do it either. Women need to embrace their uniqueness, not overcompensate for it. Don't impersonate a man. Be a full person. Gender isn't relevant to your leadership style, so stop behaving as if it is.

Complaints that women are poor delegators don't stem from chromosomes. They come from women not wanting to screw up because they're afraid they'll never get another shot.

The difference in leadership styles between men and women is an opportunity disparity, not a gender disparity. In the same way mothers do things for their children because it's easier and faster, women often choose not to delegate and instead just handle things themselves.

When this happens in the work environment, however, it hamstrings women. By simply doing the work themselves, they rob themselves of the opportunity to become effective managers. In the moment, it seems like getting something done right now is more important than how we manage our people. That is short-sighted. You may complete one project a little faster by not delegating, but becoming the best manager you can be will serve you and the women coming up behind you for far longer. Consider it an investment in yourself and other women.

The complaints that women are passive, ineffective leaders don't come from chromosomes either. They come from society imbuing women with a systemic lack of confidence and exposure to meaningful criticism.

Men have been leaders since the beginning of time. They've been in the arena, getting their asses beat, winning and losing, and they've gotten a lot of feedback in the process. As such, they've developed thicker skin in the workplace. If something doesn't go their way, they don't ruminate over personal deficiencies or wonder how they caused it. They're more likely to see a problem as external, not internal, lessening the impact of failure on their sense of self. Women could learn from that.

Part of developing thick skin is becoming comfortable with the idea that not everyone is going to like you. Separate criticism into two groups: things that belong to you and things that don't. If you hear criticism that rings a little true, listen to it, and make changes. If it sounds like someone is venting or dumping their shit on you, leave it. That doesn't belong to you. Mainly, understand that some people are just not going to like you for reasons you may never know or be able to address, so stop trying. It could be that you remind them of an old girlfriend who hurt them. It could be that they're jealous because everything seems easy for you. That is none of your business, so why let it take up space in your head? If you're a woman in a hurry to develop rhinoceros skin, try sharing a controversial opinion on social media or blogging about current events. You'll reach your goal in about a week.

To become effective leaders, women must reject what society tells us about our abilities. Since we were little girls, adults told little boys to be gentle with us, or do things for us. Women have internalized this message and believe that they are weak, ineffective, and less capable. Reject that. There is simply no basis to believe it.

When women fall into this belief, I ask them to do an exercise. Go back to the beginning of your life and inventory your successes. Go through the bad thoughts you're experiencing– self-doubt, disappointment, shame–and replace that space and energy with your accomplishments. It can be something as simple as remembering the time you found a wallet and tracked down the owner to return it. It could be the march you lead in high school against gun violence. It could be the day you got into college, bought your first home, got a promotion, or finished a woodworking project. You have 100 percent control over what you allow to take up space in your head. Why not restrict that area to things that make you feel good, worthy, and competent?

The worst management style is the hybrid, passive-aggressive. This type of manager is not direct because they fear pushback, dissent, and criticism. Their intent is to get their way, not to invite discussion or consider alternatives. When faced with conflict, instead of being direct, they do an end-run around the conflict's source to attempt to enlist others in furtherance of their cause. These are the leaders who will try to convince you that people important to you are on their side and since no one agrees with you, you are clearly in the wrong. They try to break you down and manipulate you into doing what they want, and can make you doubt your most basic beliefs. The purest example of passive-aggressive behavior is when a mother tells her child "no," and instead of dealing with mommy, the child goes to daddy to try to get his way. Passive-aggressive behavior is toxic. If you find yourself engaging in it, stop, because it's damaging to your reputation, and erodes people's trust in you. You're better than that.

Become an Optimist and Dream Bigger

If you get nothing else about your mindset from this book, let it be this: become an optimist. It's a gift you give yourself. If you're not inclined towards optimism, do whatever it takes to train yourself. It's that important.

Confirmation bias is the idea that we find in the world what we seek. If I've made up my mind that all men are bad, I will find examples of crooked men everywhere. Likewise, if I believe that setbacks are just opportunities making a bad first impression, bad experiences won't have the same negative effect on me as they would on a pessimistic person who sees the set-back as proof that life isn't fair, they're not worthy, so there's no use trying. Optimism is a commitment to seeing the best in the world. It doesn't mean bad doesn't exist, just that you view it with proper perspective.

Growing up, I was always optimistic. As bad as my childhood was in many ways, I always found something on the horizon to look forward to. But I was never a *big* dreamer. Renting a bigger apartment in a nicer complex was a dream. Owning a water-front home was not. Having a job where I wore a suit to work every day was a dream. Owning the workplace was not. Being married was a dream. Being the breadwinner was not. I used to believe that I could only reach a certain level in society or a career because I didn't have lineage, breeding, or connections.

But guess what? If your mind is open, doors will open. And when those opportunities present themselves, if you don't believe you have any natural, pre-determined limits, you'll take them.

Be Prepared: With Success, Sexism

When people see you struggling alongside them, they tend to be supportive. But when you have things they want, when you reach levels that they aspire to but have not achieved, something changes in the way they look at you. Especially if you're a woman. And this comes not just from men, but from other women as well. I refer to it as a form of enhanced sexism—when the criticisms and critiques of you and your success come from other women.

The higher up I go in life, the more authority I have, the uglier it gets, and I'm more aware of sexism now than when I experienced it in more conventional ways. I get fewer misogynists catcalling and commenting on my hair and dress. The sexism I experience now isn't from simply existing as a woman, I get it more from ruffling feathers.

I speak my mind about my political and social beliefs and promote female empowerment through my platform, which reaches countless people. My speaking out has made other women feel comfortable with sharing their views and being heard. In doing this, I bump up against a long-established status quo, and the people who've always benefitted from the status quo are just about tired of my bullshit. In their view, for pushing back against long-held conventions, and worse, getting their women all riled up, someone needs to put a boot on my neck. The mere fact of my success brings out the worst in small-minded men who feel their place in the world is threatened by women like me.

A big storm came through town recently. A huge pine tree snapped in half and fell across my yard. I posted a picture of the tree online and the men working to remove it. One guy, whom I didn't know at all, commented, "Oh, the poor little rich girl's got a problem."

When people make comments like this, I used to just roll my eyes and think, *What a dick. I can't believe he took the time to post such a snarky comment.* Now, I call them on it. I embarrass them. Before long, the person clearly demonstrates why they're an asshole. See, these comments are petty, disrespectful, and most importantly these are things men would never say to other men.

In this case, I responded, "Would you say that to a man who had achieved my level of success?"

Then he began blowing up my phone, private messaging me to apologize. "I didn't mean that, Ms. Dana. I'm so sorry, Ms. Dana." Still, I didn't delete his comment, or my response, and in about ten minutes an army of women and a few progressive men were excoriating the guy. He ended up deleting the post. Now, I suspect that ruined his day. But if I hadn't put him through that, had I not been tedious, had I not allowed other people to show him the insensitivity of his remark, he'd have done it again, maybe to someone who would've just taken it and seethed quietly. Because I took the time and didn't just let it go, he had *his* day ruined, and I bet he thinks twice before he smarts off to another grown woman.

It stings even worse when a woman does this to another woman. One would hope women would be aware of their own oppression, at least enough to stay out of the way if they don't want to join the movement, but some of the most vocal opposition against female empowerment still comes from other women.

For example, a woman once commented on a picture I'd posted of my backyard, "Not all of us are comfortable with you making enough money to be able to live in (my neighborhood)." Instead of celebrating another woman's success, this woman felt it necessary to inform me that mine made her uncomfortable and even suggested that her and other people's opinion of it should carry some weight with me. I feel certain she would not have made that comment in response to my male law partner posting a photo of his beautiful backyard in the very same neighborhood.

Sexism from other women hurts in a unique way. The comment was public, for all to see, with her name on it. It was clear she felt strongly about it. I couldn't understand why my success offended her so much. I really couldn't understand why she thought I'd be concerned with whether she felt comfortable with how much money I make or how I choose to spend it. It was as bizarre as it was disheartening.

In all likelihood, her frustration came from my upsetting the applecart. I'm not staying in my lane. Change makes people uncomfortable, even when it's positive change that benefits them. Most people want to stay with the devil they know. And I get that. I've been there. When I was married to an attorney who was the predominant income earner, I experienced sexism in every important aspect of my marriage, but stayed and made the most of it, looking for reasons to stay married for many years. I wasn't looking for problems with that model, because I was so heavily invested in it.

This same mindset is how Phyllis Schlafly recruited so many women with her anti-feminist rhetoric in the 1970s. Even today, many women of all ages believe feminists are screwing up the world order for them. These women want traditional marriages. And should they divorce, they want to know they'll get child support and alimony. They like their roles as nurturers. They don't want to become ball-busting career women. That's too hard. They fear they can't do it or downright just don't want to. These women are so uncomfortable with change, they don't want any other women to experience it for fear they will necessarily have to change as well.

The functional feminist knows better than to let the frustrations of these women bother her. The feminist movement was never about converting women from one lifestyle to another. It has always been about equal opportunities to have the life you choose, including being a wife, mother, caregiver, or being unmarried, divorced, lesbian, bisexual, or nonbinary. It's about *choice*, not any particular culture or value system.

Just know that as your success grows, you may face more, not less, sexism. For the benefit of women coming up behind you, call it out, so they won't have to. Don't abide misogyny. Don't encourage it by ignoring it. Spend your time wisely. And don't let your sisters with low gender self-esteem hold you back because they don't yet love themselves as they should. You have bigger and better things to do and a less sexist society to help build.

Be Resilient

Resilience is what separates winners from losers. Not genetics, luck, or connections. How you handle setbacks and failures will determine how far you go in life.

When we get the courage to try something, and it doesn't go well, we're reluctant to try again. Once bitten, twice shy. This is especially true for women. We take failure or difficulty as a sign something is not meant to be, instead of as a sign that it's harder than we thought, and will probably be more rewarding when we achieve it. How we see failure is a choice. We can look at setbacks as learning experiences and launching platforms to greater successes, or failures and dead-ends. It's up to us.

I think of a legal analogy for processing failures and set-backs. When attorneys argue over what evidence a jury should consider, they discuss the concept of "weight vs. admissibility." One side doesn't want the jury to consider a piece of evidence, the other side wants the jury to have it. Most judges want the jury to hear everything and sort out the truth for themselves. The most common ruling, in response to an attorney who doesn't want the jury to consider a piece of evidence, is "That objection goes to the weight of the evidence, not its admissibil-ity." Just as you cannot deny the evidence that there are failures in life, you can decide how much weight you give them. Are you learning from setbacks or allowing them to define you?

Women often give too much weight to their failures and perceived deficiencies. Many believe were it not for one big mistake, deficiency, or setback, they'd have the lives they want. They say, were it not for being overweight, short, boring, divorced, married, not going to college, losing a job, taking a job, having a child, or not having a child, "my life would be perfect." They meditate on it, drowning out opportunities for success or new beginnings. That's not how you achieve.

Watch the weight you give to "failures." Was it really a failure or was it a lesson? Were your mistakes as big as you've made them? Or are you obsessing over something that wasn't a big deal until you made it one? Learn the lesson, if there is one, and move on.

The easiest way to redistribute the space and weight you give experiences is to do a replacement exercise. Practice identifying your successes and revel in them. Spend at least as much time recalling how you accomplished it, the odds you had to overcome, and how great you felt, as you'd spend ruminating on a failure or setback. Do this until you've drowned out and replaced the feelings of incompetence and negativity you felt about the failures with the confidence, joy, and encouragement you feel from all your successes. It's not an exercise in ego building, it's retraining your mind to make the most space for and give the greatest weight to what has helped you achieve your successes.

A large part of being resilient is learning how to handle embarrassment and humiliation. People often gossip about me, because I'm "famous" in my little world, and sometimes their comments get back to me. I've heard some hilarious stuff, from who I'm supposedly dating to how I got where I am. Every new rumor is more far out than the last one. I've had to become comfortable not giving my side of the story. Even if I could correct every piece of incorrect gossip about me, some people still would not believe the truth, so why bother? I became comfortable with people talking about me. I chose to let it flatter me. If anyone ever asks about a rumor, I disabuse them of false information, but I do not seek out those opportunities. Overall, it's been helpful to my brand and my business to be a topic of conversation. No, it's not fun when people outright lie about you, especially publicly, but when you're in the public arena, that's going to happen. So long as you're putting good out into the world and helping others, the people targeting you will have to work a lot harder to make you look bad. People like that tend to find easier targets and eventually give up.

Don't misunderstand me. I'm not just talking about idle gossip. I've experienced events that could have crushed me, had I not worked on being resilient. I had to learn that although some fails seem really big at the time, if I can keep my sense of humor and the right perspective, I can laugh at myself and get through pretty much anything.

For example, years ago when we first had a television show, people started to recognize me around town, and it was kind of going to my head. I went grocery shopping one afternoon in a pair of white yoga pants. I got my buggy (that's what we call a grocery cart in the South) and started up the aisles. A lot of people were staring at me, more than usual. My big head thought they all recognized me from television. When I was about halfway through the store, a lovely woman inched up to me. I was sure she was going to ask if I was that lady lawyer from television. She did not. She pointed to the back of my pants and asked if I realized I had a huge stain on them. I did not.

On the seat of my white cotton yoga pants, there was a 5- to 6-inch orange grease stain. It was a perfect circle, removing any doubt whether I had blown it right out of my ass.

Because I had.

Forever vain and always looking for short cuts, I'd been taking an over-the-counter diet aid called Alli, or Orlistat, which sucks some of the fat out of the food you eat and keeps you from absorbing it. However, it can lead to leaky stools, which I and everyone in the Publix supermarket learned that day.

I gathered my purse and the remaining scraps of my dignity, and walked out of the store. I felt bad about leaving my full cart unattended, and called the manager to say I had to leave, but didn't want the food to perish, and would they mind putting it back. He replied, "Oh we know. We saw you. We're already putting it back."

That, my friends, was a lesson in humility *and* resiliency. Because of my mindset and self-confidence, I was not only able to survive it, but laugh about and share it later.

When you share your humiliations and embarrassments with people, it's the ultimate equalizer. The more someone gives me fangirl status, the more likely I am to tell them an embarrassing story. It makes me relatable. More than that, it models how to handle those hiccups that happen to all of us. How to not give negativity more space and weight than it deserves. By laughing at myself, I get others to laugh at themselves, and is there anything better than a room full of laughter?

Actively Combat Prejudice and Hate

In 2018, I took my daughter on a cruise for Christmas. A few days in, we were leaving our cabin when we heard an announcement, saying someone on board was in need of blood and was Type A-positive. I'm O-positive, so I knew I could be a donor. Even though we had our whole day planned and this would throw us off schedule, I told my daughter we needed to stop by the infirmary to see if they needed my blood. We'd want someone to do the same for us. She agreed.

We took the elevator down to the infirmary. When the doors opened, it was standing room only. So many people had responded that they filled the original room, spilled into the hall, and wrapped around to the elevators. It brought tears to my eyes. I saw before me a sea of human beings of all creeds, colors, races, genders, ages, nationalities. Not one of them knew who they might be giving blood to, yet they'd all responded with alacrity.

They knew if they gave blood, they'd have to take it easy, drink lots of water, lift nothing and drink no alcohol for at least one to three days. That's quite a sacrifice to make for a stranger, even more so when you're on a five-day vacation. Despite all the extremism and divisiveness in the world today, one of our most basic, natural impulses is to help our fellow human.

Hate really is learned. There's nothing natural about it. But why can't we see hate forming in us and stop it, knowing it's no good? I subscribe to the belief that hate comes from homogeneity– surrounding yourself with the same, fearing and rejecting the other. Exposure to the unfamiliar is the antidote for hate. It's easy to fear something you don't understand. It's hard to hate something you can relate to.

Consider all the donors waiting in line to give blood. They never stopped to consider the worthiness of the recipient. What about the person receiving the blood? Did they tell the ship's doctor what their donor criteria were? Of course not. When your life is in danger, you don't ask things like what's the donor's religion? Is he gay? Were his parents married? How far did he go in school? How did she vote in the last election? No, when shit gets real, you're just glad there's another human on this planet who will give of herself so that you may live.

Growing up, I attended predominantly black schools. It never occurred to me not to make friends with the kids I went to school with. Why not? Still, I could tell the white adults in my life didn't think it was a good idea for me to let my black friends spend the night and borrow my clothes, or for me to hang out too much with them. The white girls who hung out with black people got a bad name. It was taboo. I had a sense the older white people in my life were watching me to make sure I didn't get too close. Having meaningful relationships with black people has provided me with insights and understanding that have benefited me my entire life. It taught me empathy at an early age but only after teaching me an ugly lesson.

When I was in third grade, our school put on a play to cel-ebrate our country's bicentennial. I was tall for my age and had red hair, so I was a natural to play Miss Kitty from Gunsmoke during the Old West portion of the play. My love interest, Sheriff Matt Dillon, was played by a little black boy. At the end of our hoe-down scene, I was supposed to end up sitting on

Matt's lap, putting my arms around his neck, giving him a peck on the lips, and exclaiming, "Well, Matt, honey, it's almost time for the BIGGGGG celebration!!!"

And I did that.

Once.

Our school was asked to perform that play for the other elementary schools as well, so it wasn't just the teachers, but the parents and grandparents of my classmates who saw it. That hoe-down scene did not go over well with other schools—at all. My teacher told me that the superintendent and other leaders were not comfortable with a little white girl sitting on a black boy's lap, putting her arms around him, and especially not kissing him on the lips. She told me to sit on his lap, don't put my arms around him, and do not kiss him on the lips, cheek, or anywhere else.

I learned that it was better to be a white hooker than a black law man.

I'll never forget how that made me feel. All this time, I'd thought my black friends were my peers. We lived in the same neighborhoods and went to the same schools. But suddenly I was being told I was different – better – in some way that I had not chosen. I was better because of something I had not earned – the race I was born into. At eight years old, that was my first understanding that as poor as we all were, it was somehow better to be white.

What was everyone afraid of? That I'd grow up, fall in love with a black boy, have his child, and dilute my race? Then what? Would the world really end? It made no sense to me. I recall that being the first time I doubted authority. The racism simply made no sense to me. I didn't see how I was any better than anyone else, especially over something I had no hand in determining. And I just didn't have any respect for anyone who supported it.

If we can learn to understand and embrace things foreign and even discomforting to us, they lose their power to cause us fear and anxiety. Anything we're afraid of, we just don't understand. Once we understand it, we can neutralize its negative impact in our lives. The same is true of people smug in their knowledge of politics and current events. Until they open themselves to alternative points of view, they don't realize how little they actually know.

Beware Complacency: Find Your Hustle

The cream will always rise to the top, but you have to stir the pot. The most successful people rise to the top because they're not content where they are. The hustler is always assessing and eliminating impediments to reaching the next level, most of which are of their own creation. The hustler gets out of their own way. They look around, see who's in the group with them, and find a way to leave them behind and move on to the next level where there's less competition. Then the process repeats.

It's a dynamic process, because when you compete at your highest level among your true competitors, you get better. It's why people don't like to play golf or tennis with people who don't play as well as they do.

Even if it's the top of a very small food chain, a lot of people get complacent once they get to the top. They tend to be the most insecure and fight the hardest when faced with a challenge. They're too invested in their status, and their fear of losing it is existential. They fear the unknown, because new information might threaten their position. Once they get to the top, they want to stay there. Their only goal is to maintain an environment in which the status quo inures to their benefit. An environment in which they are comfortable. Above these people's comfort zone is where you can shine. All of that is in play because their complacency keeps them from chasing it.

To get where you want to be, to surpass those fat cats who reached a goal, unpacked and settled in, you must become comfortable with being uncomfortable. That's where real change happens. Successful people know you have to break a few eggs to make an omelet.

Help: It's There If You Ask for It

With the right mindset, you're comfortable with not knowing everything and not having unlimited resources, although I bet you have more than you think. Coaching is hot right now because it works. It's taking the next step after identifying your problems, and deciding to make the changes necessary to improve your life.

Not everyone can afford therapy (check your health insurance, though, because it's covered now more than ever) or a life or career coach, but there are other options. There are online groups you can attend for free until you're able to pay for individual coaching. There are people in training to become coaches and therapists who run discounted or free groups, or who offer individual services on a sliding scale. Don't let the fear of paying for help discourage you from getting it. You'll find, as I have, that investing in yourself pays lifelong dividends.

CHAPTER 5

Motherhood and Freedom

Through my speaking engagements, I get the opportunity to talk with a number of young women on career development, work-life balance, and personal finance. Invariably, the discussion turns to whether and how long to work if a woman wants to have children. They often ask if wanting to take on a traditional female role makes them a "bad feminist" or a poor role model for other women and girls. They *do* want a big wedding, a strong provider husband, and to give birth to and raise their own children, yet they don't want to waste their potential or not contribute to the world outside their homes. The angst women feel over this is palpable.

I explain to them, my view of feminism is based on empowerment and free will. By coming up female in the birth gender lotto, you've likely received messages from the moment you were born that girls grow up and have babies. Women become mothers. It's the most important thing you'll ever do, society says.

Truth is, it is not your obligation to become a mother. Motherhood is not the only path to female fulfillment. It is not the only way to "become a woman." It's one of many adult options. My hope is for any woman who chooses motherhood to do so with her eyes open and plenty of preparation.

There is nothing wrong with a woman choosing to enter into a traditional marriage with traditional husband-and-wife roles where the man is head of the household so long as she realizes it financially disadvantages her and her children. Should the traditional marriage last, she will have to go to her husband for permission (i.e. money), to go, do, be, and have what she wants for herself and her children. And should the marriage end, or if her former partner is unable to provide adequate resources for the family, she will be left with a greater financial burden and a lack of career opportunities to meet it. That makes her and her children vulnerable to becoming dependent on the rest of us. The end of a marriage can put a woman and her children in an entirely different socioeconomic class.

I know it's not fun to think about. When we first start out, in love with fantasies of a happy future, we never plan for that dream coming to an end. Yet every day, dreams come crashing down, leaving women and children bearing the brunt of the financial pain. When marriages end, the higher earner, still the man in most cases, enjoys an immediate increase in his standard of living, while the women and children experience a sharp decline in theirs. What a man typically pays in time-limited child support and, in uncommon cases, alimony, is only a fraction of the financial contributions he made when the family was intact. My hope is that women recognize and plan for their vulnerabilities in all of their choices, but especially those where they turn their survival needs over to someone else.

I cannot emphasize enough the importance of having your own money. To me it's not a luxury; it's the air I breathe. It's what keeps someone from being able to put me in a cage. Even as a teenager, I understood its importance. What I didn't realize until recent years, was how much money I needed to feel secure in my own right. When you're striving to earn more, your financial goals can feel so out of reach, it's easy to want to fall back on the traditional female role of partnering with a husband who can take financial care of you. But in today's economy, that's harder and harder to find, and less and less secure if you do. The job market has changed, and our view of "providers" must change with it.

For me, even when Plan A was finding the right man, I craved autonomy, and I still do. If someone or something takes away or jeopardizes my agency, I panic. The worst feeling in the world to me is being under someone's thumb. Being voiceless. Without your own money, you don't have the power to ensure your own safety and security or your children's. You are dependent on someone else's mercy and grace. And people change. Believe that.

My primary goal as a functional feminist is for women to feel empowered to make their own decisions, with their eyes wide open. Even when a traditional stay-at-home role is available to a woman and she chooses it for herself, I want the decision to empower her. I want all women to feel their choices empower them, but for that to happen women must make informed decisions. Although many women desire marriage and traditional families, I hope when they decide what they want for their lives, it's their choice, not their only option. Regardless of our core values, the world has changed dramatically since traditional marriage seemed like a good choice for women.

In the past, men could find long-term jobs that paid enough for their wives to stay home to raise the children, with enough money left over to build savings, own a home, put their kids through college, and retire at 60, maybe with a small second home. The men stayed in those jobs their entire careers, in most cases retiring after 30 years. But there are few jobs like that anymore, especially for a blue-collar, working man. Our economy has shifted from manufacturing to services. Factory jobs are dwindling, and unions are disappearing. Most government jobs are now privatized, pay nowhere near what they did in the past, and don't have the employment protections or benefits that they used to. Bottom line: When the economy changes, social constructs must also change.

Today, most women must earn an income, because the family cannot survive otherwise. Women have to bridge the gap, earning the needed household money that the husband's sole income does not provide. Something changes in the relationship dynamic when both parties are earning, or when the woman out-earns the man. Little of the traditional marriage model feels right anymore. When the man brought home the paycheck, he received tremendous deference. The woman handled the children, made a peaceful home, and covered the bases while the man played golf, poker, or worked in his shop. But when both are working outside the home and all of their income is necessary, women rightfully expect help with all those domestic responsibilities.

For a woman of childbearing age today, deciding whether to stay home or go to work isn't the binary choice it was for women now in their 40s and 50s or older. Now, women know they're almost sure to have to work because they or their households need their income. If they can find jobs that enrich their lives, great, but the primary goal is getting a paycheck. Yet many women still want a traditional home and to be the primary caregiver for their children.

I am here to tell you, you can do all of that, with or without a partner. But you've got to be smart about how you allocate your resources. You have to look for and act on opportunities when they come your way.

Work Through Your Old Wounds

If you do choose to become a parent, be cognizant of your own childhood wounds that you're bringing forward. Resolve them, neutralize them, do something to manage them. Don't let a hard experience from your past blow up and cause a problem in the present. Be aware that what you say and do to someone during their childhood may define how they see themselves and how they interact with the world for the rest of their lives. We'd all love to have children if we didn't have to get them through childhood.

My approach to old wounds used to be to just leave them in the past. When I was very young, my parents had a physically and emotionally volatile relationship, and I was exposed to every part of it. I recall being in a constant state of feeling afraid. Feeling insecure. As if these two adults did *not* have their shit together. At all. Once I became an adult, I turned those memories off. I said, "Oh the hell with all that. Flush it." I convinced myself I'd put my difficult upbringing behind me and set about creating my own family, something I'd felt deprived of as a child.

Soon enough, those old wounds reared their ugly heads. Because I'd left them unexamined, I'd carried them with me into adulthood. Now, in addition to being a new parent, I had to manage my unresolved history, while hoping to protect my child from having to deal with any of it.

The risk of not working through your old wounds is that you burden your child with them. This is not only inappropriate, it adds to their already difficult task of growing up. Understand this about parenting: It is a one-way street. You give. If you get something back, it's a bonus, but parenting is giving. You don't have a child to be your peer, savior, or someone to love you.

If you create a good human being, a contributing member of society, then man, you have gold medaled in parenting. But it is never about them making you feel fulfilled or happy. You've got to work through your old wounds yourself and leave your child out of it.

Being a Single Mother Means Using All Available Resources

The good news is that a single mother raising a child today, with no child support or male income, doesn't have to have the same experience my mother did. When I was growing up, my mother had two choices. If she wanted to go to college, she had to go on welfare, meaning she couldn't work. If she didn't go to college, she could get a job, but with limited opportunity for advancement, and no help with healthcare or childcare. She just had to plow along.

Today, there are more resources available. Even in the late-90s when I returned to college, there was safe, on-campus childcare with enrichment activities for my daughter, so I could take night classes. There are options for women to continue their education through loans and grants, going to community or state colleges, and enrolling in work-study programs. Paid internships are more common. There's all manner of assistance that didn't exist for my mother, but by no stretch of the imagination does that mean it's easy.

Even when there are resources available to pay for school and childcare, many single moms are too damn exhausted and over-scheduled to make their own education a priority. That is when it helps to literally go through a cost-benefit analysis to help determine what the best payoff is for the limited time and resources you presently have. Sometimes that reveals a one-, two-, or five-year plan to achieve your educational goals, but make no mistake about it, having a plan is what helps you reach your goals. It's not a race, but you do have to start. That's the most important part.

Remember that education can be formal or it can be gained by keeping your eyes open and maximizing every opportunity to learn that comes your way. Resources that help single mothers build their careers are out there. The challenge is great, and the road is hard, but if you look for education, experience, and opportunity, I think you'll be happy with what you find. You don't have to find all the support you'll need all at once. Find just enough to get you through to the next level.

Be Aware of Sexism in the Home

I have bad news for you. Your daughters and your sons are being taught to look at men as more competent than women. Society programs this in every single one of us, and believe it or not, women reinforce it. In our *own homes*. Even children with feminist mothers believe men are more competent and capable than women. It's woven into the fabric of our lives.

Well, so what?

If the only reason for continuing to do something is because it's always been done that way, then ditch it. If it doesn't serve you right now, today, get rid of it. That includes outdated gender roles and expectations.

This is why feminism in the home is critical. Feminism at home means making sure your children see you as a competent, capable woman. Stop saying, "Ask your dad to do your science fair project with you." Stop saying, "When dad gets home, he'll hang up that picture." Stop saying, "We need to ask daddy," as if your status as wife and mother is nothing more than that of a senior child. Constantly deferring to a man reinforces sexism in the home.

Sexism is more pervasive when it occurs in the home. That is where we get our noses rubbed in it. When you realize the sexism happening in your own home, you go, "Oh my God, I just thought I was dealing with these assholes at work," or "I thought I was just getting demeaned when I'm trying to get my car serviced." No. If you don't pay attention, your children may grow up thinking men are more competent than women because of how they see their parents interacting in the home. Soon enough, boys start expecting girls and women to get in line, for them to let things go the man's way. Girls start looking for men to solve their problems. It's not rational to think your kids are going to be feminists if they don't see feminism embraced in the home. This wasn't always clear to me. This type of sexism was so silent, yet so pervasive, I didn't realize how much of it was happening inside my own home.

I took my daughter to London when she was a teenager. We'd been to Europe before as a family, and my husband typically handled the passports, boarding passes, plane and train transfers, and other logistical items. This time it was just us two. They speak a form of English in London, so I felt sure I could muddle through. On the flight over, I put my wallet in the seatback pocket in front of me, so I wouldn't have to dig for it every time I wanted to buy a drink. Well, when I woke up and it was time to deplane, I forgot all about the wallet.

Flash forward to us waiting for our luggage to go through customs. It was taking forever and we got thirsty. I reached for my wallet to buy a drink and felt an immediate shock through my body. I'd left it on the plane. Right away, I looked for help to radio the plane, to get someone to retrieve it and meet us in security. It was a whole big production, but I'd made up my mind I was getting that wallet back so there was no way that wasn't going to happen. What struck me was the look in my daughter's eyes the second I told her I'd left my wallet on the plane. She was *scared*. She thought we were stuck in a foreign country, all alone, with no money. In her face, I saw that she didn't trust me to keep her safe.

In that moment, I realized that in my own home, my child had learned to see a woman as less competent than a man. She'd never been fearful when my husband was with us, even when he'd also lost his wallet and identification. She had inherent confidence in his ability to handle anything that happened to us. As she was growing up, I'd figured it was easier to not argue with or contradict my husband and just let him have his way most of the time. I didn't realize my child had taken that as evidence of my having less knowledge, competency, and capability compared to him. My strategy of just trying to get along and have peace in my home had modeled to my daughter that I didn't matter as much, my opinions weren't as valid, and that I (and therefore all women, including her) was *less than* my husband in every significant way. I realized that had to stop immediately. My daughter needed to see her mom be strong.

So, I didn't just *handle* the problem with the wallet, I made sure she saw me work through it calmly and logically. I made sure to give her enough information that she would feel safe. I explained to her that if it was too late, and the plane had taken off, we'd contact the office and transfer some money or order another credit card by overnight mail. We discussed how to cut-off credit cards in situations like this, so no one else could use them.

By showing her what it looked like to be calm in a foreign land, think rationally and consider all resources available to us, I showed her she could do those things for herself and not assume her dad or another man needed to swoop in and rescue her. As she grew into young adulthood, I continued being mindful of teaching her these life lessons. There was no way I was going to raise a woman who thought she was not equal to a man. Turns out, that was an effort well spent. A few years later, my daughter, Whitney, was driving at night and came upon a girl whose boyfriend was beating her. She instinctively inserted herself into the situation and yelled at the girl to, "Get in the car! Get in the fucking car!!" The girl got in my daughter's car, crying, and my daughter drove her somewhere, helped her calm down, and just sat with her and talked to her for a long time. She told the girl, "Don't take that shit. No one deserves to be treated like that. No one deserves to be abused."

They both knew not to wait around for a man to rescue them because it was a man who put them both in danger that night. It was a very dangerous thing for Whitney to do. It took faith in her convictions and her own competency to save that girl that night.

I was asked recently what was my proudest moment. I explained it wasn't graduating law school, becoming a partner, or writing this book. It was the moment I realized I'd help produce a strong young woman willing to risk her own safety to help another woman when she badly needed it. Whitney has done a lot to make me proud to be her mother. But never have I been prouder of her than I was that scary evening she made another girl feel loved.

Parenting in the New Age: Tough Love is Out, Empathy is In

Over the last 100 years, the expectation for women as mothers has evolved, with the last 10 years showing the most rapid change. Baby Boomers' fathers were largely farmers or business owners. Their mothers handled child rearing and supported their husbands. This didn't change much with Baby Boomer women, although some did work outside the home, at least part-time, to augment the family income. Broadly speaking, the women of this generation who led the second wave of feminism were anomalous. Career women still were uncommon.

Generation X saw women enter the workforce straight out of school and remain there over an entire career. Their cohorts saw only poor or affluent women stay home with their children. Most mainstream moms needed to work. As a result, women started getting help raising their children from daycare centers, after school programs, and in-home helpers.

In contrast, for the most part, Millennial and Generation Z women know they have to work, often two or more jobs, regardless of whether they have a partner. This makes traditional parenting challenging. Today, there has to be a more equal division of child rearing responsibilities in couples. Women going it alone need to find outside support. Mothers today are less likely to have a retired or non-working parent available to watch their children while they work. If they can't afford child care, they have to form a network of people to help, or pursue a profession with more flexible working hours. With so many struggling with college debt, buying a home seems almost impossible. They can't imagine paying over $1000 a month for daycare alone.

As a result, fewer woman are interested in having children, and those who are, look for alternative parenting options. Fortunately, they're smart, and their lack of deference to traditional values and roles gives them the agility to find innovative solutions. We need them more than ever, because not only is being a parent getting harder, so is being a kid.

Children today have active shooter drills in school. Children as young as pre-kindergarten run through exercises preparing them for someone busting into their classrooms and spraying their tiny bodies with bullets. What parent is prepared for managing that level of anxiety in a child so young? Professional counselors can't even do that.

When children are old enough for cell phones, they discover the ugliness of the internet and social media. Bullying isn't taking your lunch money anymore; it's making a video of you on your worst day go viral. Sexual predators posing as concerned friends lure lonely kids into life-risking situations. Even when we monitor their media and phone use, the truth is we don't always know what's happening to our kids online or in person. We need a network of other mothers to keep their eyes and ears open and come to us when our kids are in danger.

Our children have more anxiety and depression than past generations. Why wouldn't they? They have exposure to more than we did at their age and don't have the emotional maturity to process it. Our girls still experience body-shaming, only now it's from unattainable beauty standards promoted in real-time by online influencers, not static, posed photos in fashion magazines. And that's just what we know about. We have no idea what's in the texts and snaps we never see. If we don't know what people are exposing our children to, we can't help them adjust to it. Sadly, suicide attempts and completions among young people have increased. So many times, we hear parents say they knew their child was struggling, but didn't realize how bad it was. So much happens beyond our awareness. Our children are overwhelmed and lack sufficient coping skills to manage it.

My hope is by being more intentional and present in how we parent our children, we can help them overcome their generation's unique challenges or at least functionally adapt to them. Even if you're sitting right next to each other on the couch, you're not showing up for your child if you're both on your phones, occupying two different worlds. That's not intimacy; that's proximity. Old-school parenting doesn't work on new-age kids. Empathy does.

This means reframing expectations for our children and trying to see things from their viewpont. You have to be comfortable with your kid taking two extra years to graduate college. You have to be comfortable with a gap year, or a kid who says, "I just don't want to be a parent." In the end, you've got to be comfortable with them failing by your definition of failing, because by their definition, they're not.

There is no easy path for our children. We have an ingrained belief in a specific path—high school, four years of college, maybe grad school, then getting married, having two and a half perfect children, a pair of dogs, and starting a community garden. All these things we put on our children don't apply as much anymore. And it puts our children under a tremendous amount of pressure. It's not reasonable to put the same expectations on them, given the wildly different universe in which we're living now. They're already saddling the pressure they put on themselves, they don't need any more from us.

That being said, we can't make it too easy for them, either, and believe me, I get how tempting that is. Because my childhood was so unstructured, and often dangerous, I overcompensated when I first became a parent. I ensured my daughter had a highly structured life, and I did things for her she could have done for herself, trying to give her the childhood I never had. While this comes from love, it's not in the child's best long-term interest. Fortunately, parenting styles can evolve over the course of a child's upbringing. The parent you were when your child was born should be different from the parent you are when they're a kid, a teenager, and an adult. As hard as it can be to watch, we have to let our children struggle. That's how they learn the lessons we never get the chance to teach them.

This means accepting that happiness isn't the only goal. Sometimes people have to be in pain to grow and become better people. We get upset when our children aren't beaming with happiness. We think that means we failed as parents in some way. But that's not parenting. Parenting isn't worrying about what our children project about us to the world. It is putting our children's interest before our own and letting them learn for themselves.

Sometimes people need to experience that life can suck. In the long run, these experiences help us be kinder to each other because they teach us what it's like to be on the downside of life. And more than anything, isn't kindness what we want from our kids? I often think of hard times in my children's lives as kind of like a wildfire. Once everything bad has burned, the good, healthy stuff begins to grow back. Same with the world around us. The good of humanity grows from the ashes of the bad.

No matter how tempting it is to take the bullet, don't protect your children from the consequences of their choices. If they don't take the softballs, don't take the bat and hit it out of the park for them. Let them strike out. Otherwise you're going to be taking care of them the rest of your life. And you're not going to live forever. Besides, you're hurting yourself, and when you hurt yourself, you hurt them. We didn't pop out of the box knowing what we know, like how to build credit and balance a budget. Somebody taught us. When our kids don't know how to do something, they're not stupid, they're ignorant. Do everything for them, and you'll be doing it forever.

CHAPTER 6

Balancing the Scales

I t's hard for women to get ahead on their merits when they're walking uphill the whole way. Carrying a 100-pound backpack. In heels. We don't start out on an even playing field. All the advantages go to whomever got there first, which is almost always men—the white ones.

Men got to Congress and the state legislatures first, so they've made the bulk of the laws. They got to the courts first, where those laws are interpreted. For 244 years of "freedom," a man has controlled the federal executive branch. While we have more women legislators, jurists, and governors than ever before, it's still a fraction of what we need to achieve full parity in representation. I'm not suggesting that be the goal. No, the goal should be female predominance with male accent pieces. Just think of what we have now, flip it, and give that 244 years. If it's not better, *then* consider going 50-50. *That's* fair.

Seriously, women have got to be innovative. We've got to be agile. The belief that the way we've always done things is the only way to get ahead is part of why we haven't gotten any further. Women need a collective cognitive behavioral reboot.

Watch that Mouth, Lady

Let's begin by checking our self-talk. Listen to the messages you're sending yourself. Listen to the external messages you're accepting and internalizing. Pay attention to how many times you think things like: *It's not worth it, life isn't fair, this is fine, this is as good as it gets, that life isn't available to people like me.* It starts there. Once we get control of those faulty beliefs, there's nothing to it but to do it.

We get a lot of comfort from clinging to long-held beliefs and viewpoints. It's our natural tendency to assume other people would behave the same as we would under the circumstances. If we don't like or wouldn't want to do something, we tend to assume most others feel the same way. That's just not true. When you step outside your comfort zone, meet different people, and hear varied points of view, you open your eyes to just how much untapped potential there is in the world. There is more than one way to skin a cat and more than one way to see the world.

Do Not Disparage Any Woman

Pledge today to always build up other women. Make a commitment that even when you can't find something to celebrate about another woman, you refrain from disparaging her. That doesn't mean you support positions or arguments you disagree with. It means you restrict your criticism to substantive issues and never make ad hominem attacks. In a nutshell, promise to never, ever, be a *Mean Girl*.

We need similarity to feel a deep connection with other people. I identify as a woman, and see myself on the women's team. I want it to be a winning team. If it isn't winning, I don't abandon my team. I replace the coach. I recruit new talent. I get feedback from my teammates and make adjustments. But I never ever abandon my team.

Why don't more women root for their own team? It's unnatural to pick another team over your own. It's why people are fanatical about hometown sports teams. For example, I'm a triple Seminole, meaning I have three degrees from Florida State University. If I rooted for the University of Florida Gators, you'd think I was nuts (and where I live, it's actually a misdemeanor). Yet women fail to root for their own team almost as a matter of course.

If women made up their minds to collaborate with other women instead of seeing them as competition in a male-dominated world, we wouldn't have a male-dominated world anymore. We have all the power we need to change our condition; we just don't maximize it. Worse, when we don't play for our own team, we minimize it and devalue it even further.

If women don't respect other women, why should we expect men to? We begin with self-respect. No one will respect you if you don't respect yourself. Rather than working out and starving yourself to keep your husband faithful, a comically futile endeavor, commit to eating healthful foods and getting sufficient rest and exercise to maintain optimal mental and physical health *for you*. Create goals you can achieve through your own success, not your association with someone else.

Going broader, stop overvaluing men and undervaluing women. Stop buying the bullshit about yourself and your gender. It's simply not true. I recall being in a pre-trial conference with three women on my side, and three women on the other side. Now, I would go on vacation with every single one of them. I respect them and enjoy their company. It charged me up that women lawyers litigating at the highest level dominated the entire courtroom. I loved it. But in the moment, I hated all three of them. I wanted them to lose everything they wanted. I wanted to win 100 percent. That's my competitive spirit.

But it was nothing personal. We'd all live to fight another day. Not unlike Democrats and Republicans, we find ourselves opposing each other all the time. It used to be because of differing core values we were working to advance. Now it's a fight to the death, not because of philosophical or policy differences, but for no other reason than being the "other." That (hopefully) does not mean we're mortal enemies. It just means we have important differences we're willing to fight over. This should never turn us against each other as human beings. It should never divide us.

Whether it's the Real Housewives, a football team, or a political party, it seems part of human nature to seek a cause to advance against all others. To have enemies. To be at war. That feels like a male concept to me. I believe that the more women leaders we have, the less destruction we will see. After all, we get nothing for it. Or at least not enough, considering what it costs us. The time has come to let go of outdated social constructs, and there are perhaps no constructs more detrimental than those that keep women divided.

Now that I've "made it," I make a deliberate effort to look behind me and pull up other women. All I ask is that for each woman I pull up, they have five women they're pulling up, and each one of those women I expect to have five women they're pulling up. This is not my original idea. I've observed other women making this pledge as well. In this way, a quiet revolution is taking place through countless women leaders across the world.

Hire and Refer to Women

I ask all the women I meet to pledge to try to only refer business to other women. When installing a pool or building an addition on your house, see if there are any female contractors first. When your neighbor asks for a referral to a doctor, accountant, lawyer, insurance agent, or HVAC repair person, commit to sending them to a woman. You may not know women in those fields, but at least look. Try to find them. And yes, I realize most people would be more comfortable with the most experienced or highest reviewed vendor, but those are almost always men, again, because they got there first. But that's a narrow viewpoint. Women are smart and have enough natural insecurity to not want to fail. They work harder because they know people are testing and underestimating them. They also tend to ask for help more, because the end result is more important to them than their ego. When I refer someone to an inexperienced woman, I make sure to help that woman myself. I mentor her. I link her to others with more experience who want to help her. And in no time at all, these hardworking, smart, resourceful women rise to the top.

For those of you worrying that this will cost men work and hurt their families, I get that, but this is the United States of America. We are capitalists. Women have families, too, and nowadays they're frequently the head of the household. Even if a woman lives alone, only socialism would expect her to receive less pay for equal work simply because her male cohorts had bitten off more responsibility than they could chew. Paying men more or giving them greater economic opportunities because of their familial obligations has been an outdated idea for half a century. It is simply un-American. We eat what we kill in this country. We don't expect society to pay for our families and obligations when we can't. At least not for very long, anyway.

Navigating Your Network

People get overwhelmed when they think of networking. They envision interminable lunches and mindless cocktail hours listening to boring stories, killing themselves to try to stay interested or contribute or gain something valuable. But if you can get your head straight and be of the right frame of mind beforehand, you can maximize what you get out of each social interaction. Here are a few easy things to remember as you're building your contacts.

First, don't let a person or group of people shut other women out of a conversation. If you have the power, give it back to other women in the conversation who may need it. They'll remember you for that and, with enough support from you and others like you, they'll be in a position to help you one day.

Second, give yourself sincere compliments. It will make you exude positivity, which will make people want to be around you. If you're uncomfortable in social settings, starting with low self-confidence doesn't make it any easier. So, take a minute to clear your head, think about what you hope to accomplish by being there, envision it happening, and run down that list of accomplishments and good deeds you've done. Take a minute to do a quick inventory of everything you like about yourself. Go into that room with a warm smile and bright eyes and show the world why they ought to love you.

Third, use whatever platform you've got to promote other people, especially women. It's the cheapest way to advertise. When you promote other people, they appreciate it and thank you for it, effectively promoting you themselves. By your supporting them, they will recognize you and go on to encourage others to participate, thus benefiting a greater number of people. The more people you touch, the more people whose lives you improve, the more resources you'll have when you need them.

Use Resources Wisely, Especially Time

When I mentor women, one exercise I ask them to do is to identify the resources they already have. I tell them to list five resources in their lives right now that can help them reach their goals. Then I ask them to take inventory of what they have on their calendar and assign a value to it, asking, "what do you get for this?" They often find that the things they spend the most time on are not the most enriching activities. In fact, they're often the greatest impediments to their success. Beware the time sucks you get nothing for. Conversely, if you find you have a lot of time, decide how much of it you're willing to dedicate to your goals and what you think you can get in exchange.

Leveraging your time, even on a *pro bono* basis, can lead to amazing opportunities. I have a friend with a master's in public health, who found she didn't enjoy working in that field. She loves clothes, fashion, travel, hair and makeup. Now she's a major influencer and earns her living hosting podcasts, webinars, Facebook Live, and red-carpet events, in addition to putting out her own original content. She made the time to master social media while pursuing other interests. At first, she did this for kicks, but before long, she had raving fans. Once you have a following, it's pretty easy to monetize that fanbase with people and businesses who want help promoting themselves and their products. It's how Kylie Jenner became the world's youngest billionaire at 21.[2]

Sometimes my mentoring sessions are with people who have plenty of money, but can't seem to get control of their lives and reach their goals. Extra money has obvious value, but you have to be willing to invest some of it in yourself to get where you want to be. It's how the entire concept of coaching came about. Paying people to help you stay organized or focus on a goal. Sometimes it's helping people maintain mental, physical or spiritual health. If you have money, there are more people than ever ready to help streamline your life and motivate you to follow your dreams.

If you don't have extra money lying around, don't fret. Every day there are new groups popping up in communities dedicated to helping women start businesses. Go online and you will find communities of goal setters and personal and physical

---

2 https://www.forbes.com/sites/natalierobehmed/2019/03/05/at-21-kylie-jenner-becomes-the-youngest-self-made-billionaire-ever/#152fd42794ae)

fitness coaches. There are even apps for this. You can afford them because they're often free or low cost because their creators already learned to monetize their services and get paid by sponsors. Resources are out there and a good mentor can help you find them.

Find a Mentor, Be a Mentor

We all get by with a little help from our friends. No matter what you're struggling with in life, there is somebody out there you know and respect who has dealt with that problem before and can help you manage it.

Asking for help is yet one more way to leapfrog and make up time. Why make every mistake yourself or reinvent every wheel? Learn from others' experiences and build on those lessons in a way unique to your style and values. It's not about emulating someone else's success, but rather looking for shortcuts to get you where you want to be. But to have a mentor, you have to get their attention and ask them for help.

I'd been an attorney for about five years when I received an email from an enthusiastic first-year law student from my alma mater. At the time, we had a legal call-in show on the local CBS affiliate on Sunday nights, and were advertising on television, billboards, and in the phonebook, so it was common for people to come up to me in public and talk about the show or compliment our ads. When I started reading the email, I thought it was another note from a fan, but it was much more than that.

Dana Brooks

From:	Alana Brean ████████████
Sent:	Monday, January 10, 2011 8:58 PM
To:	Dana N. Brooks
Subject:	Contact From Website
Importance:	High

Contact From Website

Name: Alana Brean
Email: ████████████
Phone: ████████████
Address: ████████████████████████
         ████████████

Comment or Question:
Dear Ms. Brooks, My name is Alana ████ and I am a 1L
entering my Spring Semester at Florida State Law. I have been
lucky enough to find my niche early on in law school (due to a
wonderful torts professor, ████████), and I have chosen the
path of personal injury law. I attended undergrad here at Florida
State as well, so I have seen you on commercials, along with
the rest of your law firm, for the past 4.5 years. I always saw
you and said "Dana Brooks is exactly how I want to be when I
grow up", I am not even exaggerating in the least bit. Ever since
seeing you on WCTV law call, you have more or less been my
motivation. Throughout the years of me being called "legally
blonde" and feeling as though both my gender and my
appearance initially provide some with skepticism of just how
serious I may or may not be, I always felt as though I relate to
you; a determined young woman who can "hang with the best of
them". I graduated Cum Laude from Florida State University in
2010, and made the Dean's List each semester from Sophomore
year onward. I then went on to receive a partial scholarship to
Florida State University, and here I am today! The purpose of
my email is to inquire into any internship position (paid or
unpaid) that your firm may have available. I am mainly focused
on having an internship for the Summer, but the only thing I
have going on right now is school, so if need be, I could start
ASAP. The reason why I have targeted you and your law firm is
because all of the pieces seem to fit. Your highly personable
attitude and familiarity with the community, are two attributes
of yours I aspire to have throughout my life. I know that you
focus on medical malpractice and that is precisely the area of
personal injury law that I find most interesting. I believe that to
get into personal injury law you have to have a genuine care
and connection with your community, and from the brief times I
have been able to catch you on television, that attribute truly
stood out. I would want nothing more than to work at the law
firm of ████████████ Fasig & Brooks. I can't imagine a
better way to solidify my career path as a personal injury
attorney than to begin at such a reputable law firm, working
under an attorney I feel has been an inspiration to me (the fact
that you, too, went to Florida State University Law School lets
me know I am the right path in my career as well)! I am sure
you and your law firm are extremely busy, but I do hope you

1

118

...ake me into consideration. I have a finalized resume, and though I have not been provided with my class rank yet, I am sure they will be released promptly. Thank you so much for your time and I look forward to hearing from you! Sincerely, Alana

Alana's email was the perfect way to get my attention. It was disruptive, memorable, and contained a call to action. She wanted to work with me, even if she had to do it for free. She knew to first get her foot in the door, then become irreplaceable, which she promptly did. My partners thought she was sucking up to me, but I saw more than that. She wanted to be where I was, and to get there, she needed to learn how. Why not ask one of the few tall, attractive, blonde women she's seen do it?

There are far too few women lawyers in ownership positions in law firms available to bring up young women behind them. I'd been so busy making a name for myself, I hadn't noticed how few women mentors there were. I was used to not having one, so it never occurred to me to be one. Looking back, my God, how much nicer – easier – it would have been to have had a strong female mentor. Instead, I was thrown in deep water without a life jacket. Still, I learned to swim – with sharks – pretty quickly. Because I had to.

For almost two years, Alana was my law clerk, meaning she did most of the legal research and writing (the mental heavy lifting). Because of Alana's tenacity and refusal to accept no, she got an up-close and personal look at private practice for a woman lawyer in the most competitive area of the law—plaintiff's personal injury. Like me, she used her experience to hit the ground running right out of law school, and is now a successful plaintiff's trial lawyer in South Florida. Not once did she shy away from or try to diminish her physicality. The reference to Legally Blonde in her email was about her looks, not her career choice. Alana is a very tall, curvy, beautiful woman with about three feet of gorgeous, long, blonde hair. She is conspicuous.

A couple of years ago Alana and I attended a trial college together. While I saw immense value in the way they structured their trial presentation, I could not have been more offended by their suggestions for how to present the case. Basically, it was an acting class, which is the exact wrong way to try a case. Jurors can smell inauthenticity. Being anything other than your true self in a courtroom is a recipe for disaster.

When it came time for Alana's presentation, the course leaders critiqued her on everything that was uniquely Alana. These were people she respected, so I could see they were starting to make her doubt herself. I stopped her in the middle of the presentation, told her to stop listening to those people (all men, naturally), and remember how many cases she's won—remember all the people she's helped through the toughest times of their lives. She didn't have to impersonate anyone else's version of a lawyer to do that. She did it by being her incredibly unique self. But those messages that "you're not good enough," or "you're not okay just as you are" come at women all day every day. The only difference was that these were less subtle.

I don't care how competent a person is, they can always get overwhelmed or doubt their choices. When Alana doubts herself, she calls me, and I pump her back up. I hope to be able to do that for her for the rest of our lives. She is like a daughter to me. Like my own daughter, I am immensely proud of her success and character, although I'm not sure how much of that is attributable to me.

Part of what Alana has taught me is there are as many benefits to being a mentor as there are to having one. When someone looks to you for guidance, you're accountable to them. Guiding another person brings out the best version of yourself. Within that, it's important for people who look up to you to see you struggle. A mentor is a model, so let your mentees see you deal with conflict and lose your cool.

Alana was the first person to inspire me to mentor women and girls. Since 2011, I've mentored countless girls and women struggling with everything from whether to start a family, complete a degree they have no interest in, or start and grow a business. From my perspective, these bright women have so much to offer, they just need to crowd out the external negativity and give more attention to their successes. I have learned from Alana and so many women like her that just one comment I make to them, just one suggestion, can be the catalyst that changes their lives. That's an awesome responsibility. I still receive emails today from women thanking me for advice I don't even remember giving. That's the power of being an influential person at the right time in someone's life.

In 2017, I got a call that presented me with a chance to help other women, 3.8 million of them. A colleague from Jacksonville was on the other line, asking if I would be the "face" of a lawsuit he and his law partner were contemplating, which would ask the courts to declare Florida's "tampon tax" unconstitutional. It was no longer an issue that directly affected me, as I hadn't needed a feminine hygiene product in over six years, but when I found out what the tampon tax was, I got fired up. Under this law, Florida taxed sanitary products as "luxury items." All those years my three teenaged daughters and I had needed them, our home state had placed menstruation in the same category as a 90-minute hot stone massage. I had no idea. Because most people never noticed the tax, much less questioned it, this antiquated law (no doubt enacted by men) had cut into Florida women's pocketbooks each year to the tune of several millions of dollars they shouldn't have had to spend. I gave my colleague an enthusiastic "yes," jumped in with both feet, and set about bringing as much attention to the issue as possible, using every contact, asset, and outlet I had.

It was a long, hectic journey building support against the tax. I put my name on a pleading and sued the governor and the state of Florida to stop the tampon tax and refund some of the money it had taken. I embraced monikers like "pink lawyer" and the "tampon tax lady lawyer." I posted, blogged, and squawked about the issue to anyone who would listen. Feminist law professors, legal vloggers and bloggers, and women's groups around the country and the world interviewed me about it.

In these interviews, I spoke to the monetary effects the tax burden had on women, the flaws in the law, and the injustice of punishing women for an unavoidable and beneficial fact of human biology. Women already earned only 77 cents for each dollar a man earns, but under this tax, they had to stretch that so much further. The law hurt poorer, more vulnerable women most. Sadly, some women try to stretch their dollars too far because they can't afford to change those products as frequently as they need to and end up with life-threatening medical conditions as a result. I attacked the law's "luxury item" argument with vigor. Luxuries are a personal choice; women cannot opt out of menstruating, and their use of sanitary products is for the health of society as a whole, not just themselves. Women use sanitary products and practice good menstrual hygiene to keep *others* safe. We don't need protection from our own blood. The very thought that women were expected to pay for sanitary products was offensive, the thought that the state would tax them as a luxury item wass infuriating.

Unfortunately, the state of Florida had bastardized the law so many times, burying it in the bureaucratic processes of so many different departments, it was impossible to tease out the errors that supported our argument for its unconstitutionality. The courts dismissed our lawsuit. But the law did change—through shame. Because of our constant promotion, news releases, interviews, and press conferences, two female legislators introduced bills to change the law and remove all taxes on sanitary products. It passed with an overwhelming majority. Never underestimate the power of shame when you use it strategically and for good cause.

Our lawsuit may have failed in the courts, but it succeeded in the outside world. It sought to recover the preceding three years of sales tax collected on sanitary products, about $45 million, and refund it to Florida women, after deducting our attorneys' fees, of course. Well, that didn't happen. But the pressure it put on legislators to act did result in $15 million a year staying in the pockets of Florida women who have never needed it more.

When I started this journey, 38 states still taxed sanitary products. Now only 20 states do, and more women and allies are shaming them for it every day. Until 2017, women in federal prison still had to purchase feminine hygiene products. Today, they are free. The overwhelming number of incarcerated women are housed in state prisons and local jails where they still have to pay for feminine hygiene products or make due with severely restricted access, often just 5-12 free pads a month and no tampons at all. If they aren't indigent inmates, meaning they have more than $5.00 in their canteen account, they often have to purchase these essential products at inflated prices, an expense a male inmate never encounters. Some have resorted to using toilet paper for pads or tampons and using notebook paper to clean themselves. Now more and more states and local governments are removing these shameful requirements and providing ample, free sanitary products for inmates. In 2020, Scotland became the first country to make tampons and pads free to all its citizens. Not just untaxed, but *free!*

If you ever think your voice doesn't matter, that you have to accept things the way they are, and there is nothing you can do about it, I hope you remember this story. Just get off your ass and try. Then prepare yourself for success, because I promise you, it's coming.

CHAPTER 7

A Note to Men

Just prior to the COVID-19 lockdown, I hired a dating service. With my face plastered all over town, joining an online dating service is out of the question. I get plenty of attention, both wanted and not so much. What I needed was help sorting through the options. The service I hired offered to conduct a thorough assessment of my unique needs, wants, and developmental stage to get a firm idea of what I was looking for. We did this through several telephone and Zoom interviews. This service was expensive, so, naturally, I felt encouraged.

Fast forward to my date with my first "match." It was on Zoom at 7:00 p.m. on a Wednesday. I actually did my hair and makeup and wore a cute outfit for this virtual date. The man they'd matched me with was average-looking, which was fine because I had expressed to them that physical attractiveness was low on the list for me. I'm into a man's mind. We chatted briefly, and I soon learned he was in no way matched for me. He exhibited none of my must-haves – no children in the home, big on travel, exceptional sense of humor, extremely positive outlook on life.

Finally, the conversation turned to me writing a book on Feminism. I explained that I thought the word had gotten a bad rap and needed rebranding to be more inclusive. I said I thought we needed the support of men to change our condition, so I included a chapter called, "A Note to Men" hoping to get them to reconsider their thoughts on it as well. He asked me a few more questions about my motivations for writing the book. We talked about what each chapter covered, and how I'd experienced feminism throughout my life, from hearing mother's viewpoints on it when I was a girl, to how I've made promoting it my life's mission.

When I was done, he just blankly looked at me and said, "Huh. So just the one chapter for men, then?"

That is why this chapter is so important to me to include in this book. Women and men don't try to understand each other.

What *Is* a Man?

I have lots of interesting life stories, but the crowd favorite is usually the one about the guy throwing up on me in the back of a plane. I was coming back from an expert deposition in Cleveland, sometime in 2012. As I often do, I was wearing all white: silk shirt, jacket, pants. This guy, I'd watched him get obnoxiously drunk at the airport bar, was *hammered*. It was late in the day, and I was sitting in the very last row, right by the stinky toilets. Drunk Guy plopped down in the seat right in front of me and reclined, so I could enjoy him in my lap for the next two hours. I remember thinking, "*Well, at least he'll pass out.*" And he did.

When the bell dinged as we began our descent, Drunk Guy woke up and started wobbling towards the bathroom. He was clearly disoriented. He stopped a second to gather himself, then started to sway side to side. I remember thinking, "*Don't you do it. The bathroom is right there. Don't you dare."* Well, he dared. He retched. All over me. I was covered in vomit. It was in my *hair*.

This immediately infuriated a couple of men sitting in our area. They all threw down in fisticuffs. I got caught in the crossfire, and one of them ended up punching me. I'm the original victim, but because these guys were so furious, they hit me trying to … I really don't know what. Get retribution for stinking up the cabin? Defend me from a vomit attack?

When we arrived in Atlanta, the authorities were there to arrest Drunk Guy, but I still had to take the last flight from Atlanta to Tallahassee. The stores were closed, so I had to take a sink bath in the women's room and do my best to wash whatever used to be inside a drunk man's belly out of my Elie Tahari suit. It was a long day.

By traditional gender norms, the response of the men around me was reasonable. They saw a threat to a woman, and acted on instinct to protect her. I believe this comes from a lifetime of societal conditioning: you're bigger and stronger. You can kill with your bare hands. Your main job as long as you can remember has been to protect. Whether it's through providing for your family or knuckling up in an airplane, you must protect the weaker sex. As women, we think so much about how you guys want to control us, but I wonder if from your perspective, it's really protection you're aiming for, albeit sometimes misguided.

Men, it's time to examine the role society has conditioned you to take. Is it true to you, or did society force it upon you when you were young, and you've never questioned it or experienced any otherwise? Does your view of being a man help you, or harm you?

Women, it's time for us to rethink whether we need our men to protect us. Don't they have more to offer than just a paycheck or forcibly addressing any threat we face? Don't they also need protection? For ages women have been disappointed in men because we think they only see the world from their perspective. That they have no empathy. But can't the same be said of us? How often do we try to consider things from any perspective than our own? I'd like us to consider why men behave the way they do. If we look at it closely, the male gender role is often as destructive to men as it is to women.

From the preceding six chapters, you may have arrived at the assumption, falsely, that I hate men. I describe a tremendous number of flaws in their treatment of women, children, and the world. Is that why I wrote this book? To make the case that women are awesome and men suck? Not at all. I love men. In fact, I'm famous for it. I've been married four times to three incredible men, all of whom I loved, and was at one point eager to spend the rest of my life with. I do not believe all men will disappoint me, and I certainly hope they don't believe that about me.

What I do believe is that we are not inherently weak and you are not saviors, providers, or protectors. You're just people. Peers and potential partners. And I believe you have shouldered an *enormous* amount of social expectation in pursuit of the all-important goal of being a "real man." Personally, I would hate that expectation. I never struggled with not feeling like a "real woman," probably because I had a child. But I know many women who have chosen to remain childless who get a tremendous amount of grief about it from other women. It is heartbreaking to see women not support each other in that one very important aspect of their lives. You guys are so much better at that than we are. We could learn something from your sense of brotherhood.

The idea that gender is something achieved by behaving in a "real" way was flawed from the start, and now it's outdated. It simply doesn't serve us anymore. More and more women are ready to ditch these antiquated gender norms, and men should be too. Imagine a world where two partners, regardless of gender, are in it together. Where each has an opportunity to be their unique, true self. A world where one of them isn't disproportionately advantaged or disadvantaged because of gender, and neither has to bend over backwards to "achieve" womanhood or manhood. That is a world I'd love to live in.

The Pressure of Being a Man

From the time you are born, society tells you to be gentle and protective around women and children. When you're old enough, society tells you to choose a wife, start a family, and provide for that family until you die. As far back as you can remember, society tells you, "Girls are weaker, take care of them. Don't let anybody hurt your sister. Don't let anybody disrespect your mother. Protect. Provide. Protect. Provide. If you're weak, you're not protecting or providing, and therefore not a man. If you cry, or enjoy music or the arts, or display any hint of femininity, you're showing weakness. Show weakness, and you fail as a man."

This is a crushing amount of pressure to put on an adult, let alone a little kid. I'm impressed at how some of you have been able to cope with this pressure without becoming complete and total assholes. But even those of you who manage live less-fulfilling lives than you would without the constraints of your traditional gender role. Just like women, men also want to leave unfulfilling, sometimes abusive relationships but feel too much pressure to stay. Just like women, men also want to leave a boring job and start a new career or open a business that you enjoy that changes the world. Don't your dreams matter, too?

My trainer's wife unexpectedly died, and it sent him into a tailspin. Once everything settled down and he regained his footing, he bought himself a little Mazda Miata. He's a very frugal man. He explained that his food bill had obviously decreased as well as other forms of consumption so he felt he could justify the purchase. He was very positive about it and I could tell the car brought him much joy. But it made my heart hurt. I realized that for 30 years this man's default, his M.O. every single day, was to put his wife first. Whatever she needed and wanted took priority over anything else. He could have afforded that sports car ages ago. But he didn't indulge himself until his children were grown and out of the house and he no longer had the responsibility of providing for his wife.

That's how ingrained it is for many of you to put your families and your women first. I've only lived in the American South, so maybe this varies by region. Still, we read the same books, we watch the same television and movies, and we get the same news. Wherever you are in the world, society tells you that if you aren't a provider and protector, you aren't a real man. It makes me wonder whether the pushback on gender equality isn't about you not believing we're as capable or as competent as you are so much as it's about you not understanding where or how you'd fit into any other world.

It makes sense then, when a feminist doesn't respect or acknowledge the challenges and sacrifices men face in their traditional role, that a man might say, "Fuck a feminist. If a feminist is just going to make me feel like everything I've done in my life is worthless, then fuck a feminist." I understand why feminism has a bad rap with men. Again, a degree of empathy is missing, this time on our part.

Feminists Don't Hate You

In the 1960s, 70s, and 80s, feminism took a more hostile attitude towards men. And for good reason. You had almost complete control of the opportunities available to women. You were obstacles in our path to equality. This is where the false stereotype of feminists as "man-haters" took root. To be sure, there was a fair amount of man-hating going on. While this attitude was far from unfounded, it sent a threatening message.

For the sea-change our society needs, we need feminists of all sorts, including men, which means a lot of empathy needs to occur. We need to appreciate that we're all coming from a good place, and let go of our gender assumptions. In my experience, rigid gender roles don't help you guys any more than they help us.

It's Not My Gender, It's My Life

The more we women take on roles that are traditionally male, the more you're going to see different behaviors in us. Most of what we consider male behavior isn't based on gender, it's based on circumstances. When we own and run businesses, we are going to demonstrate behaviors typically associated with men. That's because we have responsibilities now that used to be almost exclusively held by men.

Take drinking, for example. For years, you've had the responsibility to run companies, provide for your family and sometimes even your family's family. It's a lot of pressure. Men have long relieved stress with a drink here and there. Now, as more of us women are climbing the ladder of success, we're also enjoying a cocktail or two along the way. The increase of drinking in women is through the roof. That's because there is nothing gender-based about wanting to ease stress.

Another example, we are louder and more opinionated now. We speak up and expect to be heard. You men have a lot more opportunity to fail, so you learn early on how to get back up and try again. Believe me, once we get enough experience with it, our skin gets just as thick as yours.

Men who cling to outdated gender roles often find women like me threatening. I display traditionally male behaviors. I don't stay in my lane. I am not ladylike. I speak directly and maintain eye contact. I drink, and I'm louder than other women, even some men. I can be a bully. (I'm working on that.)

But I've found that when a man finds a woman's behavior irksome simply because of her gender, he is a low-quality man. Men of quality are never threatened by women of equality.[3] A quality man is self-effacing and challenges his assumptions when he feels triggered. A quality man has more in his bag of tricks than simply doubling down. A quality man is a smart man.

---

[3] That's not my original thought but someone needs to put it on a t-shirt.

Most of our assumptions come from basic miscommunication, misunderstanding, and a lack of empathy. We often make assumptions about you based on our culture, our education, or what experiences we've had with other men in the past. You seem to make assumptions about us based on gender roles, past experience, and often, your own unexamined insecurities. In the long run, the only people who benefit from these assumptions are those interested in maintaining them. If we let go of our assumptions, if we learn and grow, then we all win.

Redefining the Male Role

The financial and moral pressure of the traditional male gender role as it exists today is staggering. When I consider what you must think of when choosing a mate, I'm frankly shocked that any of you ever get married. For generations, society has taught that becoming a husband means financing an entire operation of people's needs: spouse, children, and sometimes parents, in-laws, and grandchildren. Daunting doesn't begin to cover it. No wonder you guys don't run around getting your couple initials monogrammed on everything. You're probably sitting in a corner somewhere with a calculator figuring out how much you've got to earn and how long you're going to have to work to pull this off. At first, I imagine you're scared shitless, not overcome with marital joy. I can't help but think you'd like a little help with all that pressure, beginning with an acknowledgment that it actually exists.

I've found if given the option, a lot of you would opt out of the traditional male role. Many of you already have. Many of you only want to be responsible for yourselves and having children scares you more than it interests you. I see more and more men looking for peers and partners, rather than dependents. Many of you who do opt for families participate more – sometimes equally or better – in the caregiving responsibilities.

Refusing to accept traditional gender roles benefits us all. Women gain access to the power we always should have had, and men get the tremendous relief of releasing yourselves from traditional male expectations. Let that shit go. For this to happen however, we need to redefine what success and failure look like.

This shouldn't be a tough sell. If you have less financial pressure to provide for your wife, and less moral pressure to protect her, because you know she is not weak, you'll probably lead a more enriching life and live longer. With more time and energy, you'll be closer with your family. You'll treat your wife as a peer instead of your eldest child. You and your partner can share the burdens and responsibilities of caring for your children and parents. Maybe you can take a month off every year now, or take up a sport, or travel more. If I were you, under this new paradigm, I would think my ship had come in.

Redefining male gender roles makes partnership possible in a way it otherwise wouldn't be. I had a friend recently change careers after 30 years in banking to get into financial planning, a big risk that he was able to take because his wife is an accountant and they had a partnership. They strategized and planned that transition together.

The fewer obstacles there are to taking risks, the more risks people will take. For example, if a couple knows they have healthcare covered, the more likely one of them is to start a business and create jobs instead of remaining an employee of a company just to maintain benefits. Taking that risk doesn't just help that couple, it helps society as a whole.

For women, redefining male gender roles is a no-brainer. Not only does it lift a big boot off our necks, it opens the door for the men in our lives to offer greater support. There are now many men saying, "I will take that supportive role. I will be your house manager. Your assistant. Your help with the kids. Whatever you need, so you can focus on all the things you do better than I do, which is generate more income and help more people."

Until that cultural change occurs, the hardest part will be fighting our conditioning. When a man chooses a different role for himself, like being a stay-at-home dad or homemaker, society's program still interprets that as if he's lazy. A loser. I don't care how evolved we think we are; we're just not used to seeing it. It's a double standard even I struggle with.

Part of me thinks of that man, *You're not reaching your potential. You're not performing as you should. Everything is stacked in your favor, so why aren't you taking advantage of it?* That is our deeply engrained societal conditioning trying to reinforce traditional gender roles. As feminists, we women have to understand that we don't get to pick and choose the consequences of a new world order. Just as you must become comfortable with us taking on different roles, so too must we become comfortable with you changing roles as well.

A Call to Action

The women and girls in your life need you to have their backs. I use the word "backs," because they do not need you to have their fronts, as a shield or a guide the way the old, paternalistic school of manhood would have you believe. No. There's a difference between supporting and protecting.

I heard a news story in July of 2020 about the Black Lives Matter protests in Portland, Oregon and the "Wall of Moms" that had gathered to form a barrier between the protestors and the police. Upon seeing the police using teargas on these women, a group of men arrived with leaf-blowers, and stood *behind* the Wall of Moms to blow the gas away. It worked surprisingly well. Critical to their response was *how* they did it. They didn't go to the front of the protest and step out ahead of the women who were on the front lines. They weren't there to diminish the women or shield them from the police. They were there to *support* them. They literally had their backs. This is what a male feminist looks like.

Each day, more men are joining the ranks of feminists the world over, in ways big and small. They're helping raise a generation of empowered girls and equitable boys. They're teaching their "bros" about consent, and how no woman is safe until all women are. They're giving up their unearned privilege wherever they can, in the name of a better world. They're fighting the good fight, without ever making it about them.

Women and men need to come together like never before. Men need to support women's equality, and women need to support men in nontraditional roles, or respect their choice to remain in normative male roles. Everyone has the right to self-determination, as long as they make informed and voluntary choices. Too many times they aren't. All too often, men and women accept what they think they have to tolerate because they know no otherwise. I invite you to learn otherwise. Your life will only improve.

About the Author

Dana Brooks is a trial lawyer with a passion for protecting and promoting women and girls. She uses her platform to bring light to issues facing women in all aspects of their personal and professional lives. Her law firm, Fasig Brooks, has won the Tallahassee area's People's Choice Award for Best Law Firm eight years in a row. She is proud to say the firm has 57 percent women partners, and is 75 percent women-owned.

Before becoming a named partner at Fasig Brooks, she served as a paralegal, law firm administrator, clinical social worker, and Florida Supreme

Court-certified family law mediator. She formerly served as president of the Capital City Justice Association, and currently serves as a member of the Florida Bar, the Tallahassee Bar Association, the Florida Justice Association, and Tallahassee Women Lawyers, among others.

Dana is the recipient of numerous professional and civic awards, including the Tallahassee Women Lawyers' Rose Deeb Kitchen Award, which recognizes female attorneys who have overcome significant adversity and obstacles to becoming an attorney. Named by the *Tallahassee Democrat* as one of the 25 Women You Need to Know in 2021, Dana is a featured speaker at many conferences on the subject of women's advancement in the workplace, and is co-creator of the popular local television show, Come Back Stronger. She has one daughter and lives in Tallahassee, Florida.

Made in the USA
Columbia, SC
05 December 2021